SIENA

City Guide-book and map tourist itineraires

PUBLISHED BY

officina
grafica
bolognese S.R.L.

info@ogbsrl.it

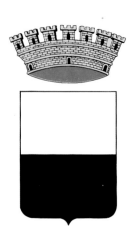

SIENA

Introduction

At first sight, this marvellous city stretching out before the eye of the tourist, looks like a huge terracotta-coloured patch on the landscape, studded with soaring spires and surrounded by strong Medieval city walls. Siena spreads out over three hills in the middle of the Tuscan plain, bounded on either side by the banks of the rivers *Arbia, Elsa* and *Merse*. The slopes on which the city is built converge in a wonderful shell-shaped concave, that is *Piazza del Campo*. The city contained within the walls has maintained its Medieval charm, thanks to the pains taken by the townspeople to preserve their heritage and to continue to keep their traditions alive; traditions which are expressed in the world famous *Palio*. The walls are interrupted at intervals, by city-gates which give access to the city by the most important roads, namely *Porta Camollia* which leads to Florence, *Porta Romana* which leads to Rome and *Porta S. Marco* which leads to Grosseto. Other characteristic features of Siena are the springs into which water from the clayey ground under the city was channelled. The oldest and greatest source of water is contained in the *Fonte Branda*, which is situated at the foot of a spur of land on which the *St. Dominic's Church* is built. *Fonte Gaia* which can be found in the upper part of *Piazza del Campo* is also very beautiful. Other springs or fountains, although less well known are of equal interest and they are *Fonte Ovile, Fonte Nuova* and *Fonte Follonica*.

The Historical Background

As legend would have it, the oldest part of the city was founded by Remo's sons *Aschio*

and *Seno,* who had fled to Siena to escape their uncle Romolo. This theory is backed up by the emblem of the city which depicts a *she-wolf* suckling twin boys. Another legend attributes the foundation of the city to the Galls from "Senones", who stopped here on their way to invade Rome in the 5th century BC However, it is certain that Siena was inhabited by the *Etruscans,* a theory proved by the discovery of numerous archaeological finds which date back to the 2nd century BC. In 20 BC, Siena was conquered by the Romans under the command of Emperor Augustus who founded a military colony, called *Sena Julia,* here. Siena then fell into the hands of a succession of different rulers, beginning with the Longobards who lost it to the Franks and was eventually, during the 11th century AD, taken and governed by the *Count Bishops* who in turn gave it up to the rule of the *Consoli,* a lay government which substituted the previous clerical government. Under its new masters, Siena reached the height of its political and economic glory entering into direct competition, for purely economic reasons, with its neighbour, Florence, which was in part Guelf, because

Siena had provided a safe-haven for the Ghibelline fugitives. Siena, reached the climax of its importance in 1260, when at *Montaperti*, it defeated and decimated the Florentine Army. This epic battle was commemorated by Dante in the X° Canto of his work "Inferno" or "Hell". After this splendid victory however, a period of decline set in, caused by internal strife between the nobles of the city over the excommunication of the Ghibelline Family of Siena by the Pope. Many of the leading figures of the city changed sides, because of this, giving their allegiance to the Guelf Family and establishing the *Council of Nine* which presided over the city until 1355. This period witnessed an artistic fervour which gave rise to many of the most important city monuments among which is the *Palazzo Pubblico, the Torre del Mangia, the Fonte Gaia, the New Cathedral* and the seven kilometre long *City Walls*. Most of the major fountains and almost all the historical buildings, both public and private, which exemplify the Senese-Gothic style today, were also built around this period. However, the incessant rivalry between the different economic factions together with the consequential internal squabbling which ensued, weakened the city drastically. As a result, Siena fell into the hands of the Viscounts only to be taken over by the Petrucci under whom the city enjoyed a period of relative stability. This stability, however, was short lived, and on the death of Pandolfo civil strife burst out once more and culminated in 1530, with the arrival of *Carlo Of Spain* who then ruled until the Spanish were expelled from the city in 1552. In 1555, Florence under the guidance of *Gian Giacomo dei Medici*, finally managed to put an end to the centuries of rivalry between the two cities of Siena and Florence in a final victorious battle which forced Siena to submit to her age-old enemies who added the city to the *Grand Duchy of Tuscany* which was passed from the Medici family to the Lorena family. At the end of a period of Napoleonic domination, the city was once more, restored to the leadership of the Lorena family who remained in charge until 1859 when Siena was first considered as a Tuscan city and later, after a plebiscite was carried, out it became part of the *the Kingdom of Italy*.

Spectacular aerial view of the Old City

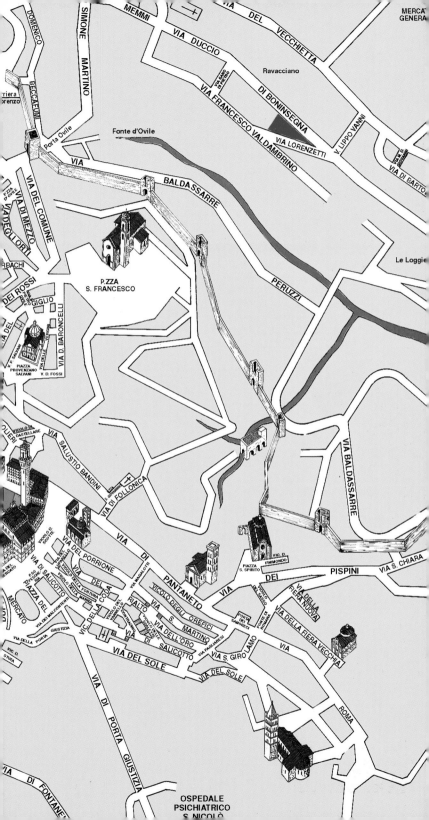

The Artistic Background

Although Siena has never enjoyed the patronage of any one particular noble family, but was, rather plagued by rivalry and fighting between different factions (factions, however, that were quick to bury the hatchet when it came to improving their city artistically), Siena, holds within its walls a surprising number of masterpieces of all kinds, from architecture to paintings and from sculpture to the minor arts such as miniature gold-smithery, decorative artwork and pottery. The greatest part of Siena's heritage dates back to the beginning of the 12th century when *Romanesque Style* made a deep impression on architecture, as seen in the *St. Peter at the Magione Church*, *St. Donato's Church*, *S. Quirico's*, *St. Mark's and St. Christopher's*. Examples of the expression of *Gothic Style* which was refined into *Siena-Gothic Style* by the creative genius of native born artists, can be seen all around Siena. The *Cathedral*, best represents the passage from Romanesque to Gothic architecture. Work on the Cathedral was begun in the 12th century but continued over a period of two hundred years. The *Palazzo Pubblico*, is the best example of Civil Architecture of the Siena. Gothic Style that there is in the city and was the inspiration for many other buildings, among which the most noteworthy are the *Palazzo Sansedoni*, *Palazzo Chigi-Saracini*, *Palazzo del Capitano*, *Palazzo Marsili* and *Palazzo Buonsignori*. Even in the field of military art Senese art reaches

levels of excellence, as the visitor can verify by observing the city walls, the city-gates and the fountains generally found in the vicinity of the walls. The so-called *Siena Arch* is a classical example of this style with its blind archway surmounted by a pointed Gothic arch. At the beginning of the 15th century the Florentine artists *Bernardo Rossellino* and *Giuliano da Maiano* together with architects from Siena, *Antonio Federighi* and *Baldassarre Peruzzi* introduced the first characteristic features of *Renaissance Architecture* to the city of Siena. Evidence of this style can be seen clearly in the *Palazzo Piccolomini*, and in the *Palazzo della Papessa* (Abbess' Palace), in the *Chapel of the Square*, in the *The Pope's Lodge* and also in the *Palace and Chapel of the Devils*. In the Baroque period *Damiano Schifardini* was in charge of the construction of the *The Church of St. Mary of Provençe* while *Flaminio del Turco* planned the construction of the *The Churches of St. Peter and St. Paul*. With regard to the field of sculpture, Sienna boasts a beautiful *pulpit* by the artist Nicola Pisano and the *statues* that decorate the front of the Cathedral by *Giovanni Pisano*, but the Siena sculptures par excellence must be those of *Jacopo della Quercia*, who sculpted the *Fonte Gaia* and the *Baptismal font* in the Baptistery. However, it was to be on canvass that the true expression of Art in Siena, in all its uniqueness and force was to have its greatest success. One of its pioneers was *Guido da Sienna*, whose master-

pieces can be admired in the *Palazzo Pubblico*, where there is his *"Madonna eseguita"* which dates back to the second half of the 13th century. The real founder of Senese painting is considered to be *Duccio da Boninsegna* whose work completed between 1278 and 1319 has come down to us in the form of the *Maestà* in which the grand master manages to marry the remnants of Byzantine art to Early Gothic art. Following in their footsteps, the artist *Simone Martini, Ambrogio* and *Pietro Lorenzetti*, were responsible for creating a school which produced other illustrious artists like *Taddeo di Bartolo, Lippo Vanni* and *Barna*. The tradition of Siena art was carried on through the following centuries by masters like *Sassetta, Vecchietta* and *Giovanni di Paolo* of the 15th century, while a century later artists like *Sodoma, Domenico Beccafumi* and *Baldassarre Peruzzi* took over. After these golden years of Senese Art, the city fell into the hands of the Spanish and later under Florentine dominance, which marked a period of artistic sterility, especially as the *Medici* family had already created a Tuscan art centre in their own city of Florence.

1: *Panorama*
2: *Via di Città*
3: *The State Archives: The Good Government in the Gabella office, by Benvenuto di Giovanni*
4: *Palazzo Pubblico, Sala della Pace (Room of Peace): The Effects of the Good Government on the City, by Ambrogio Lorenzetti*

THE PALIO

The origins of this popular pageant which is the fruit of a whole year's work and preparation for the *Contrade,* or city districts, and indeed, for the whole of Siena, are to this day unknown. It seems as though the first Palios were held after the battle of *Montaperti* against the Florentines in 1260, as a festival of thanksgiving to the Virgin Mary for the decisive victory won by the people of Siena. However, it was not until 1310, that the Palio was officially marked on the state calendar as an annual event to be held every 16th August in honour of the *Virgin Mary.* In 1656 the *Palio delle Contrade,* in honour of the *Madonna of Provençe,* which was held on the 2nd July every year was officially recognised. The various town districts or quarters were once, more numerous and were reduced to the actual 17 *contrade,* in 1729, by decree of *Violante di Baviera,* then governor of the city, who divided the city into three *Terzieri* or thirds, *City Third, St. Martin's Third* and *Third of Camollia.* This is the way the city is divided even today. Each *Contrada,* or district has its own headquarters, its own church apart from its parish church, its own museum where the famous *palii* or banners are on display along with other mementoes. It also has its own general assembly, which represents the whole population of the area, and whose job it is to elect its own *Prior,* every two years along with a *Capitano* (or Vice Principle) who are responsible for the smooth running of the *Palio.* Each year only ten *Contrade* are allowed to participate in the *Palio,* while the seven excluded districts have the right to participate the following year running. The other three *Contrade,* are chosen, at random in the *Palazzo Pubblico,* from the ten contestants of the previous year, to make up the number. The *Gonfaloni or colours* of the three additional *Contrade,* chosen are immediately hung from a first floor window, while the original seven have their colours hung from the windows on the second floor of the building, before the extraction of the three. The days leading up to the two *Palios,* are frenetic for the inhabitants of Siena who throng the streets and squares for the traditional blessing of the horses and the ceremony of the choosing of their riders. Each *Palio* is preceded by a *Historical Pro-*

cession of the Districts which files out in front of the *Entrone* before the horses and their riders. The climax of the festival is the long-awaited race which begins when the *Mossiere* (flag-man) drops the *Canapo* (flag) and is soon finished after three hair-raising rounds of the *Piazza del Campo,* at break-neck speed. In this way the work of an entire year finishes in a matter of minutes but for the people of Siena who have the *Palio-fever* in their very veins, it has all been worth while. For them days, spent at meetings or making arrangements or on bets on who is going to win and also sometimes bitter discussions are not in vain.

1: The people crowd into the Square
2: The start or "mossa"

CITY THIRD

The Noble Contrada of the Eagle

The emblem of this contrada is a two-headed eagle with an Imperial crown over its head and a sun on its chest where the letters U.I. stand out. King *Umberto I Savoia* bestowed these letters onto the Contrada in 1887 when he attended the Palio. The flag is yellow with black and blue lines, and the Contrada's headquarters is in *Via del Casato di Sotto* directly opposite the *Church of St. John the Baptist dei Tredicini* which in 1788 was named Oratory of the Contrada.

Contrada della Chiocciola (Snail)

A sliding snail in the centre of silver shield surrounded by rose buds and the initials U.U. is the emblem of this Contrada. The colours of the flag are yellow and red with blue threading, the headquarters is in *Via S. Marco* in the adjoining rooms of the *Church of St. Peter and St. Paul*, the Contrada's Oratory since 1816.

Contrada Capitana dell'Onda (Flagship of the Waves)

Represented by a crowned dolphin rising from the sea, the original colours of the banner were black and white to be then changed to blue and white in 1714. The Contrada's headquarters can be found in *Via Giovanni Duprè*, next to *St Joseph's Arch*, which was donated to the Contrada in 1717 by the *Granduca Pietro Leopoldo*.

1: *The parade of flag wavers before the Palio*
2: *The Palazzo Pubblico with the flags of the Palio*

11

Contrada della Pantera (Panther)
A crowned rampant panther that stands out from a silver shield is the coat of arms for this Contrada. At the top of the shield there is a red square with the letter U, and the flag is coloured red and blue with white lines. The Oratory of the Panther is the *Church of St. Quirino and St. Juliet*, whilst the headquarters can be found in the same street.

Contrada della Selva (Forest)
Here we can see a rhinoceros standing at the foot of a leafy oak, while the top part of the coat of arms portrays a golden sun on a blue backdrop with the letter U. The colours of the flag are green and orange with white lines. Since 1818, the Oratory and the headquarters of the Contrada have been in *Piazzetta S. Sebastiano*.

Contrada della Tartuca (Tortoise)
The coat of arms depicts a tortoise surrounded by daisies and House of Savoy knots on a golden field. The flag boasts the colours of yellow and blue, whilst the headquarters and the museum of the Contrada are in *Via Tommaso Pendola*. The adjacent Oratory was built by the locals in 1684 and is dedicated to *St Anthony of Padua*.

1-2: Two scenes from the blessing ceremony of the Contrada

Contrada Priora della Civetta (Prior of the Owl)

The emblem of this Contrada is a crowned owl sitting on a small branch. Stamped onto the black and red background are the letters U and M, and these same colours are used for the Contrada's banner. The headquarters can be found in *Via Cecco Angiolieri* and the Oratory, built by the locals in 1935, is in the adjacent medieval courtyard of the *Castello degli Ugurgieri*.

Contrada del Leocorno (Unicorn)

A rampant unicorn in the centre of a blue bordered shield with the words *Humberti Regis Gratia* represents this Contrada. The colours of the banner are white and orange with blue lines. The office and the *Oratorio* are in *Piazzetta Grassi* in the small *Church of S. Giovannino della Staffa*.

Nobile Contrada del Nicchio (The Noble Contrada of the Shell)

This coat of arms portrays a silver shell between two branches of coral and a House of Savoy knot interwoven into two Cyprus roses, topped off by a crown, all on a blue background. The banner also has blue as its main colour with yellow and red motifs. The headquarters and the Oratory, built by the residents of the Contrada, have been in *Via dei Pispini* since 1680.

1: A view of the historical procession

2: The "Carroccio" carrying the Palio

Contrada di Valdimontone (Ram)

The rampant and crowned ram stands out of this coat of arms, next to the animal is letter U. The colours of the banner are red and yellow with white lines. In *Via di Valdimontone* (the same as the name of the Contrada) are both the headquarters and the Oratory, situated in the recently restored Romanesque *Church of S. Leonardo*, and have been there since 1741.

Contrada della Torre (Tower)

A crowned elephant holding up a tower is the emblem of this Contrada. After the visit of King Umberto I in 1887, the red saddlecloth with the white cross and the small flag waving from the tower were added. Since 1500, the banner has always had a wine-red background with blue and white decorative motifs. The headquarters and the Oratory, both dedicated to *St. James*, for the past 400 years have been in *Via Salicotto*.

CAMOLLIA THIRD

Nobile Contrada del Bruco
(The Noble Contrada of the Caterpillar)

At the top of this coat of arms is the cross of the House of Savoy, whilst the emblem of the crowned caterpillar sliding on a small branch is in the centre. The colours of the banner are yellow and green with blue lines. The headquarters, museum and Oratory, built in 1680 by the locals and dedicated to *S.S. Nome di Dio*, can all be found in *Via del Comune*.

1: A scene from the uncontrolled race   *2: The blessing of the Palio*

Contrada del Drago (Dragon)

A rampant winged dragon waving a blue flag with a crown over its head is the emblem of this Contrada. The flag colours are red and green with yellow lines. The headquarters and the Oratory are in Piazza Matteotti, formerly Poggio Malavolti, and are situated in the *Church of St. Catherine* following a decree by the Grand Duke in 1787.

Contrada Imperiale della Giraffa (The Imperial Contrada of the Giraffe)

The coat of arms depicts a giraffe held by a Moor with the words *Humbertus 1° dedit* written on a blue banner above them. The colours of the flag are white and red. The headquarters of the Contrada is in Via delle Vergini, whilst since 1824 the Oratory can be found in the *Collegiate Church of St. Maria of Provenzano*, where the figure of the Madonna of Provenzano is kept.

Contrada dell'Istrice (Porcupine)

A crowned porcupine surrounded by roses and a House of Savoy knot stands out of this coat of arms. The flag has a white background with red, black and blue arabesques. The headquarters and the Oratory, dedicated to S. Bartholomew, have been in the *Church of St. Vincent and St. Anastasia* in Via Camollia since 1788.

1-2: The nervous moments before the start of the race

Contrada della Lupa (She-wolf)
The coat of arms depicts a she-wolf giving milk to twins and the *Balzana Senese*. The border of the shield contains small red and white crosses on the same colours in turn. The colours of the flag are black and white with orange rims. The headquarters and the Oratory are in the 16th century *Church of S. Rocco* in Via Vallerozzi, given to the Contrada in 1786 by the Grand Duke.

Nobile Contrada dell'Oca (The Noble Contrada of the Goose)
A crowned goose wearing a blue ribbon around its neck with a cross of the House of Savoy is the coat of arms of the Contrada. The flag has a green background with arabesques and red lines. Built in 1465, the headquarters and the Oratory are in the locality of *Fontebranda*, attached to the *St. Catherine's Sanctuary*.

1: The headquarters of the Contrada of the Goose
2: Celebrating the victorious jockey

3: The victory dinner:
guest of honour, the horse

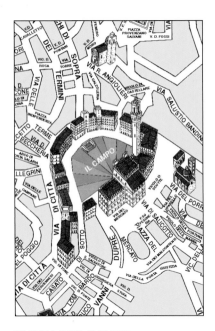

PIAZZA DEL CAMPO

This incredibly beautiful piazza is the heart of the city. It is here that the Senese have always lived the moments of joy and of sadness linked to the destiny of their city. The piazza has for centuries set the stage for the many scenes of rivalry between the Contradas during the days of the Palio.

The three hills that meet where the city of Siena is built causes the Piazza to slope slightly and the "bottom" is closed by the majestic *Palazzo Pubblico* with its mighty *Torre del Mangia*. Other splendid palaces close off the higher part of the piazza.

The semicircular and slightly concave structure of the piazza calls to mind a shell further reinforced by the fact that the central part is divided into nine segments separated by strips of white stone. Here we are reminded of the *Government of Nine*, which gave way to the paving of this part of the piazza in 1347, laid out in a herring bone of bricks, exactly like the lines of a shell.

During the Palio the horses run along the boundaries of the piazza, which are in grey stone. Due to the unevenness of the ground the shape and the paving of the piazza is irregular, creating the stupendous optical effect that makes the piazza unique in the world.

1 - PALAZZO PUBBLICO

This building is in the bottom part of the piazza and is made up of three main bodies, each with its own style. Construction began in 1288 and was finished in 1310. The prisons and the Salone del Gran Consiglio (Grand Council Room) were built between 1327 and 1342. The second floor with the two side bodies was built in 1680. The three bodies together, with the view of the *Cappella di Piazza* and the *Torre del Mangia* on the left, represent one of the most important examples of *Gothic Senese Architecture*. Originally the seat of the Signoria and the Podestà (Governor of the city), today it houses the offices of the Local Council.

The Exterior of the Building

The bottom part, which is made of stone, is characterised by a series of windows and portals closed off by the double Senese arch. The upper floors are in brick and alternated by mullioned windows with three lights, whilst the top part of the main body of the building (with two she-wolves on the sides) has a large disc at its centre where the *Monogram of Christ*, painted in 1415 by *Battista di Niccolò*, stands out.

1-2-3: Magnificent views of the Piazza del Campo

The sides of the disc has two beautiful mullioned windows with two lights, whilst the upper section is closed off with its powerful ribbing that continues into the two side bodies and contains two belfries. Between the mullioned windows of the first floor there is the *Medici emblem* of 1560 with the *Balzana Senese* next to it and its black and white shield, whilst on the other side there is the *Leone del Popolo* (the People's Lion).

The Interior of the Building

Access inside the building is through the right portal and, after having crossed a large atrium, we are in the vestibule that is divided into four bays. This vestibule boasts two stone she-wolves, the work of *Giovanni Pisano*, a small statue of Moses by *Antonio Federighi* and frescos depicting the Senese saints and blessed by *Sano di Pietro*. On the sides of the vestibule, where the offices of the Local Council are located, we can admire a splendid fresco of 1445 by Sano di Pietro depicting the coronation of Mary with Saints Bernard and Catherine and the brilliant *Resurrection* by Sodoma (1539).

1: *The Palazzo Pubblico*
2-3: *The Civic Museum: Room of Maps of the World*
4: *Simone Martini: His Great Majesty*

By the same artist there is also a fresco depicting an imperial eagle and Putti that adorns the walls of the *ex Sala dei Matrimoni* (the Marriage Room). The ceiling of the large room where the *Cappella dei Nove* (the Chapel of Nine) was once situated is decorated with frescos of a *Benedictory Christ amongst Cherubs*, whilst the other rooms boast works by *Vecchietta, Lorenzo Veneziano, Vanni* and *Salimbeni*. The stairs to the first floor lead us to the *Civic Museum* the vestibule of which houses a 1430 gold-plated she-wolf feeding her young by *Giovanni di Turino*. The fresco that depicts the *Madonna and Child* dates back to 1340 and is the work of *Ambrogio Lorenzetti*. We then proceed to the *Sala del Mappamondo* (Room of Maps of the World) so named as it once housed a large map, which has now disappeared, of the territory of Siena by *Ambrogio Lorenzetti*. In this room there is the large fresco of the *Maestà*, one of the first works of *Simone Martini* that dates back to 1315. The centre of the fresco portrays the *Madonna Seated on the Throne* with Baby Jesus and on the sides there are portrayals of 32 saints, angels and four of the Apostles, whilst the remaining eight hold up the canopy that overlooks the entire work. This work is considered one the mas-terpieces of Gothic Senese Art thanks to the great artistic flair demonstrated by Martini that gave the characters their fluid harmony. The entire fresco is framed with twenty medallions depicting Christ, the Prophets, the Evangelists, the Church Doctors, the old and the new Law (a two-faced figure) and the seal of the Republic. Unfortunately, humidity began to damage the fresco and Simone Martini himself carried out the first works of restoration after only six years. Erosion still continued and therefore today the work is in precarious conditions. To the sides of the *Maestà* are two large frescoes by *Sodoma* that depict *St Victor* to the right and *St Ansano Battezzante* to the left.

On the opposing wall there is another masterpiece by Simone Martini that portrays *Guidoriccio of Fogliano amongst the Montemassi Castles* and *Sassoforte of Maremma*. This work recalls the victory of the General, depicted riding a majestic war-horse, who conquered the Montemassi Castle after a long siege.

1: *Sala del Mappamondo: on the pillars,
   St. Catherine by Vecchietta and
   St. Bernard by Sano di Pietro*
2: *Sala del Mapppamondo: Simone Martini,
   Guidoriccio da Fogliano*

capable of combining the majesty of his subject with the simplistic linearity of the surrounding countryside, creating a very suggestive image.

Under this great fresco there is a 13th century painting, the work of *Guido da Siena*, depicting the *Madonna and Child Seated on a throne*. It is considered one of the first masterpieces of the Senese school of painting and was given its finishing touches at the beginning of the 1300's by *Duccio da Boninsegna* or one of his disciples. In the same room, high up between the arches, are two monochrome frescos portraying two victories of the Senese over the Florentines and the English, whilst the pillars are adorned with a painting of *S. Catherine of Siena* by *Vecchietta*, a *S. Bernard of Siena* by *Sano di Pietro* and a painting of *Blessed Bernardo Tolomei*, the work of *Sodoma*.

We then proceed to the *Sala della Pace* (Room of Peace), also referred to as the *Sala dei Nove* (Room of the Nine) as it was the room where meetings of the Council were held. To be admired in this room is a large series of frescos by *Ambrogio Lorenzetti* completed between 1337 and 1339 that decorate the walls of the meeting room of the Government of the city with political subjects. The frescos are considered to be the Maestro's major work and portray *The Good Government*; *The Effects of Good Government in the City and in the Country*; *The Bad Government*; *The Effects of Bad Government in the City and in the Country*.

The fresco of the Good Government portrays an old King, draped in the colours of the flag of Siena and surrounded by the *Magnanimity*, by the *Temperance* and the *Justice* to the left, and by the *Prudence*, the *Strength* and *Peace* to the right. The figures of *Wisdom*, *Harmony* and *Angels* also appear. Scenes of everyday city and country life are depicted in the fresco of The Effects of Good Government in the City and in the Country, whilst the

other two represent the Bad Government and its effects. Here we can see *Tyranny* leaning on a large, black billy goat and surrounded by *Cruelty, Deception, Fraud, Fury, Discord* and *Perfidy*. Further up we can find *Avarice, Conceit* and *Vainglory*, with Justice chained and trampled.

All the frescos are captured in a fable-like atmosphere that marks both the characters and the landscape of the city and the country.

From here, we move into the *Sala dei Pilastri* (Room of Pillars) that houses the bell of the *St. Christopher's Church*, who called the people to fight in the battle of Montaperti, two crucifixes that date to the 12th century, a coffer and other decorative pieces.

The Civic Museum - Sala della Pace
1: Ambrogio Lorenzetti: The Effects of the Good Government
2: Ambrogio Lorenzetti: The Effects of the Bad Government

that date to the 12th century, a coffer and other decorative pieces. Of particular interest is a painting reproducing on one side the *Preaching of St. Bernard* and on the other *St. Bernard Liberating a Possessed*. The work is by *Neroccio di Bartolomeo Landi*. Moving back we arrive at the *Anticappella* (Antichapel) with its magnificent fresco by *Taddeo di Bartolo* that depicts characters of Ancient Rome and Greek mythology. On the opposing wall is a painting of St. Christopher by the same artist.

We then proceed through a beautiful wrought iron gate to the *Cappella* itself (Chapel). This gate is the work of *Giacomo and Giovanni di Giovanni*, perhaps designed by *Jacopo della Quercia* and dates back to 1437. Inside, the walls and ceiling are covered in frescos by *Taddeo di Bartolo* depicting *Madonna and the Evangelists*, *Church Doctors* and *Prophets*. A beautiful marble altar by

Marrina with a large painting by *Sodoma* on top depicts the *Holy Family* and *St. Leonard*. The beautiful wooden choir stalls made up of 22 benches that run along three walls, a carved work in Gothic style by *Domenico di Niccolò*, portrays subjects taken from the *Creed*. Going back through the Antichapel we arrive at *Sala dei Cardinali* (Room of the Cardinals), with its frescoed walls with figures of *Saints* and its painting depicting the *Madonna and Child* by *Guidoccio Cozzarelli*. Here there is also a beautiful wooden *Crucifix* of the 1300's and plastered wooden statues of *St. Anthony Abbot* and *St. Ambrose* by *Antonio Federighi*.

The Civic Museum
1: *Sala dei Pilastri (Room of Pillars)*
   Neroccio di Bartolomeo Landi: St. Bernard Preaching in the Piazza del Campo
2: *The Chapel*
3: *The Chapel: Taddeo di Bartolo, frescos with stories of the Madonna*

By proceeding through an elegant marble portal by *Bernardo Rossellino* in 1448, we enter the *Sala del Concistoro* (Room of Consistory) where the walls are decorated with tapestries by *Gobelins* of the 13th century and other Florentine tapestries. The vault boasts the magnificent frescos of *Domenico Beccafumi* that portray scenes of Greek and Roman history, Harmony, Justice and *Amor Patrio* (Love of One's Country).

The *Sala della Balia* (Room of Authority), or the *Sala dei Priori* (Room of the Priors) takes its name from the fact that the *Government of Authority* held its meetings in this room. It is separated by an arch with frescos of the Evangelists, while the vaults and the ceiling, with frescos by *Martino di Bartolomeo*, are divided into 16 triangular sections, each with a figure of a *Virtù* (Virtue). The walls boast the frescos of *Spinello Aretino* and date back to 1408 and depict life scenes of *Pope Alexander III* who in fact was *Rolando Bandinelli* from Siena. The carved wooden door is by *Niccolò dei Cori* and the 1410 inlaid wooden bench by *Barna di Turino*. The *Sala del Risorgimento* (Room of the Italian Risorgimento) houses various works by Senese artists of the 19th century that portray the decisive moments in the annexation of Siena to the Kingdom of Italy. The five rooms that look onto the *Cortile del Podestà* contain a rich numismatic collection of coins and seals, and include examples of ceramics and other smaller works. Down the stairs is the *Loggia* that looks onto the rear of the Palazzo Pubblico. Inside the Loggia, bas-reliefs and original sculptures by *Jacopo della Quercia* for the *Fonte Gaia* are kept. From here, we move onto the *Sala Grande della Signoria* (Grand Room of the Government) that today houses the Council Room with its rich paintings and frescos. The other rooms of the second floor are for the conservation of paintings from the 17th and 18th centuries, prints and antique maps of town planning of Siena, its history and the Palio.

1: The Civic Museum: Sala di Balia (Room of Authority) with frescos by Spinello Aretino

2 - CORTILE DEL PODESTÀ

This courtyard was built in 1325 and restored in 1929.

The material used for its construction is cotto, like the Palazzo Pubblico, and it has a beautiful arcade.

The upper floor is characterised by large, acute arch mullioned windows with three lights.

Here, we can admire frescos from the 14th century, various emblems of the Podestà and a statue of Mangia.

1: The Loggia of Palazzo Pubblico:
Jacopo della Quercia: original sculpture
for the Fonte Gaia
2: Palazzo Pubblico: the courtyard

3 - CAPPELLA DI PIAZZA

The Chapel in the Square is to the right of the Palazzo Pubblico.

Construction began in 1352 upon instruction of *Domenico d'Agostino*, but was only completed in 1376 by *Giovanni di Cecco*.

The Chapel was built to fulfil the wishes of the Senese during the terrible plague of 1348.

The decoration of the pillars was then completed between 1377 and 1381 and in 1648 assumed its final and present look after the construction of the Renaissance arches and the vaulted roof, the work of *Antonio Federighi*.

1: The Chapel in the Square
2: The Tower of Mangia

4 - TORRE DEL MANGIA

The Tower of the Mangia is situated behind the Chapel in the Square on the right hand side of the Palazzo Pubblico and rises majestically to a height of 102 meters, overshadowing Piazza del Campo. It was named after the first bell-ringer who was known as *Mangiaguadagni* which was then abbreviated to the *Mangia*. This same name was also given to the statue that struck the hour, which was still functioning up until 1780. The base of the Tower was built of brick, between 1338 and 1348 by the brothers *Minuccio and Francesco di Rinaldo*. The upper section of the tower, including the belfry was built of white stone on a plan by *Lippo Memmi*, Simone Martini's brother-in-law, in 1341. The great bell, called the *Sunto* after *Maria Assunta*, was built in 1666 by *Girolamo Santoni and Giovanni Battisti Salvini*, whereas the clock was designed by *Giovanni da Milano* who also restored the building. To reach the top of the Tower from which one can enjoy a magnificent view of Sienna and the surrounding hills, one has to go through a door which opens onto *Cortile del Podestà*.

2

37

5 - FONTE GAIA

The Gay Fountain is in the upper part of the Piazza del Campo and was built between 1409 and 1419 by *Jacopo della Quercia*, the most important Senese sculptor of the time. Della Quercia managed to combine memories of Gothic Senese style with the Renaissance, at its very beginnings at the time, in his statues and reliefs that surround the fountain. Today, the original sculptures are kept in the Loggia of the Palazzo Pubblico, whilst the imitations that we can see outside are the work of *Tito Sarrocchi* and date back to 1868. The sculptures are held in niches and represent, from left to right: *The Creation of Adam; Wisdom; Hope;*

Strength; Prudence; An Angel; Madonna and Child; An Angel; Justice; Charity; Temperance; Faith; The Banishing of Adam and Eve from the Garden of Eden. The source of the fountain is an aqueduct of the first half of the 14th century. The name *Gaia* was given in remembrance of the joyous and gay festivals that accompanied its inauguration in 1414.

6 - PALACES IN PIAZZA DEL CAMPO

The Palazzi of Piazza del Campo are laid out in a semicircle around the upper part of the Piazza crowning it beautifully with an overall architectural harmony. The

1-2: The Gay Fountain

result was the fruit of specific planning carried out by the Governors, who, as early as the beginning of the 14th century passed a law making it compulsory for all buildings overlooking the square to have mullioned windows with either two or three lights. They also prohibited the construction of lean-to roofing or protruding galleries on all the façades bordering on the square, in order to conserve the perfect architectural harmony that we see today and to ensure that the overall effect blended in with the Palazzo Pubblico, also facing the square.

7 - PALAZZO PICCOLOMINI OR THE STATE ARCHIVES

Work on the Palazzo Piccolomini was begun in 1469, almost certainly following a plan drawn up by *Bernardo Rossellino*, who also built the palace which bears the same name, at Pienza. It is one of the finest examples of Renaissance architecture in Siena, inspired by Florentine style. The palace is two storeys high and has elegant cornices which separate one floor from the other, while elegant mullioned windows with two lights add a touch of nobility to its smooth ashlar front, which covers the entire building. The palace, is the present seat of the State Archives which can be reached through an inner courtyard. Among the treasures stored in the archives there are parchments, seals and maps of the city which document life in Siena over the centuries. The collection of *Tavolette* or tablets painted by the greatest artists of Siena were used as book-covers for texts on *Public Administration*. The surviving tablets date over an extensive period of time, with the earliest examples dating back to the 13th cent. right through to the middle of the 17th cent. They depict coats of arms, portraits of the governors of the day and also scenes from the political and religious life of Siena.

1: The Palaces as seen from the Torre del Mangia
2: Palazzo Piccolomini or the State Archives

The State Archives

1: The oldest tablet of the Biccherne collection (1258). The Papal Chamberlain is the Abbot Ugo, a monk of St. Galgano

2: The Virgin protects Siena in the time of earthquakes, by Francesco di Giorgio Martini. Detail of a Biccherna tablet - 1467

3: The Virgin recommends Siena to Jesus, Gabella tablet by Neroccio di Bartolomeo (1480)

4: The finances of the Council in times of peace and in times of war, Gabella tablet by Benvenuto di Giovanni (1468)

8 - PALAZZO CHIGI-ZONDADARI

Unfortunately, this building, situated between Palazzo Piccolomini and Palazzo Sansedoni, is only a remake of the original building. The work was carried out by *Antonio Valeri* in 1724.

1: Palazzo Chigi-Zondadari
2: Palazzo Sansedoni

1

2

9 - PALAZZO SANSEDONI

Palazzo Sansedoni is the most impressive of all the buildings in the Piazza. Its great merloned tower and mullioned windows with three lights which decorate the façade are mirrored by the façade of the Palazzo Pubblico which stands opposite it. The similarity between the two buildings, including their facings is remarkable. The original plan of the building was made up of pre-existing buildings joined together in 1216. It was later enlarged by *Agostino di Giovanni* in 1339, though the façade facing the square is the result of restoration work carried out in the early 18th cent.

10 - LOGGIA DELLA MERCANZIA

The *Loggia* was built between 1417 and 1429 for the *Corporazione dei Mercanti* (Merchant's Guild) on a project drafted by *Sano di Matteo*. It is situated at a point considered to be the heart of the city at the so-called *Croce del Travaglio* where three streets meet; *Via di Città, Via Banchi di Sotto* and *Via Banchi di Sopra*. The word *Travaglio*, meaning suffering or labour, was given to this particular cross-roads because it was the scene of frequent skirmishes between the various factions of citizens who raised barricades here to mark out their territory, often obstructing the passage way and making travelling in this district very difficult. The *Loggia*, has a façade of three large Renaissance arches decorated with niches and statues of a Gothic style, making it one of the most significant examples of the gradual change-over from one dominant architectural style to another. During the 17th century it was renovated and finished with the addition of the upper section. On the pilasters inserted into Gothic tabernacles, two statues, one of *St. Paul by Vecchietta and the other of St. Peter by Federighi* can be admired. Inside, another masterpiece by Federighi is the table on the right which represents five Roman figures. The table on the left, though executed in the same year of 1464, is the work of *Urbano da Cortona*. The back of the building which overlooks Piazza del Campo was built on a project drafted by *Niccolò dei Cori*.

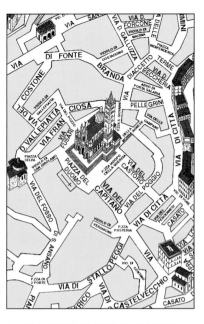

1 - PALAZZO CHIGI-SARACINI

This building was formerly known as *Palazzo Marescotti* when it was originally built in the 12th century to be finally completed during the 14th century and then restored in 1920. The façade is broken in order to keep in line with the winding street in which it is found and has the typical *Torre Senese* (Senese tower) on the corner. The ground floor of the building is in stone whilst the second floor is finished in brick and both the upper floors have beautiful mullioned windows with three lights. Large doors and ample windows set in acute curved arches are reserved for the ground floor. By wish of *Count Guido Chigi-Saracini*, the building houses the *Chigiana Music Academy* since 1932, today recognised as one of the most important finishing schools of music studies. Every year the Academy organises the *Siena Music Week,* held in July, drawing the attention of an international audience and the participation of world-famous artists. The Count has left a collection of musical instruments to be conserved in the *Sala del Concerto* (Concert Room) of the Academy. The *Galleria* (Gallery) boasts paintings of great artistic value, such as: *St. Martin, Madonna and Saints;* *Madonna and Saints*, both by *Sassetta;* *Madonna*, by *Sano di Pietro; Madonna*, by *Vecchietta; Madonna and Child, Saints and Angels*, by *S. Botticelli; Baby Jesus*, by *Perugino, Madonna Seated on the Throne with Angels and Saints* by *Spinello Aretino*, and other works by *Beccafumi, Pontorno, Sodoma* and other artists.

Palazzo Chigi-Saracini

43

2 - PALAZZO MARSILI

Even though this building was constructed in the middle of the 15th century, designed by *Luca di Bartolo*, its aspect is almost exclusively Gothic. The cotto façade of the building is further decorated by rows of mullioned windows with three lights.

3 - PALAZZO PICCOLOMINI OR PALAZZO DELLE PAPESSE

The building takes its name from *Caterina Piccolomini*, sister of *Pope Pious II*, who asked *Bernardo Rossellino* for its design and was built between 1460 and 1495. The Renaissance style of the palace includes rusticated ashlar for the lower section of the façade and smooth ashlar for the upper section. However it is different to Florentine Renaissance style as elements deriving from other styles, especially Gothic, have been used; a trait typical of many other Senese buildings. The ground floor has large portals and the upper floors are decorated with mullioned windows with three lights. A number of restoration procedures have taken place on the building; the last completed in 1864 by *Augusto Corbi*.

4 - CASA TORRE FORTEGUERRI

The house is on the corner of Via di Città and *Piazza Postierla*, also called the Four Cantons Piazza, which has a large marble column with a Senese she-wolf on top that dates back to 1487. The 16th century Palazzo Chigi alla Postierla faces onto the Piazza on

the corner of Via del Capitano. This building houses two frescoed rooms, the work of the Flemish painter *Bernardo Van Rantwick* with stucco reliefs by *Marcello Sparti*.

5 - PALAZZO DEL CAPITANO

This building was constructed in the 13th century in Gothic-Senese style, as is demonstrated by the Senese arches on the ground floor, the mullioned windows with two lights on the upper floors and the merlons. *Luca di Bartolo* transformed the Palazzo in Renaissance style in the 15th century to be returned to its original style in 1854 by a further restoration. Inside there is a beautiful courtyard, typical of the external staircase that leads directly to the upper floors. The name of the building derives from the fact that when construction of the building was completed, it housed the *Capitano della Giustizia* (Justice Captain).

1: *Palazzo Piccolomini*
2: *Piazza Postierla and the beginning of Via di Città*

3: *Via Banchi di Sopra*
4: *Via della Galluzza*
5: *Panorama*

6 - THE CATHEDRAL

History

Construction on this masterpiece began in 1229 and due to the numerous battles fought by Siena, the black plague of 1348 and various other events, was only completed over two centuries later. The original intentions for the Cathedral of Siena were to outdo the grandeur and sumptuousness of the Cathedral of Florence, fierce enemy of Siena at the time. It is precisely for this reason that many details are in different styles. The first financing came from the Council of Siena that entrusted its construction to a group of citizens of the *Opera di S. Maria* (St. Mary's Institute). In 1258 the administration of the project was taken over by the *Cistercian Monks of St. Galgano*, who called upon *Giovanni Pisano* in 1284 to substitute the façade to make it more majestic. The whole construction, with its aisleless cruciform plan, central dome and apse and polychrome marble finishing had been completed for about twenty years. Giovanni Pisano worked on the Cathedral until 1296 when he left Siena having completed only the lower section of the façade in Romanesque style with three large arches over the portals. Works were suspend-ed after his departure to be recommenced in 1317 under the direction of *Camaino di Crescentino* with the extension of the building at the apse. Works were progressing at a steady pace when the *Grand Council of the Republic* decided on a further extension in 1339 in order to rise to the levels of the great power of the city and the considerable increase in its population. According to the new project, the already existing section of the Cathedral was to become the transept of the new side construction, therefore giving it impressive dimensions. These new works began immediately firstly under the direction of *Lando di Pietro* and secondly *Giovanni and Domenico d'Agostino*. Work was again suspended in 1355 as the enormous building demonstrated problems of a static nature, but the project block was especially due to the serious financial problems caused by the black plague of 1348 and adverse political events. Once the grand project had been abandoned, the intention was to at least complete the original project. Therefore, the unfinished and unsafe sections were

1-2: Spectacular views of the Cathedral. In photo 1, notice the grandeur of the Duomo nuovo wing

demolished and the vaults were erected. Between 1356 and 1359 *Giovanni di Cecco* completed the upper section of the façade and in 1382 the apse was completed. The upper section of the façade is different to the lower section, in that it had been completed almost one century earlier by *Giovanni Pisano*. The style is in fact Gothic, even though attempts were made at combining the two styles with careful movement of the two sections. These different objectives and administrations of the various projects are the cause of the anomalies and asymmetry that can be seen. This fact does not however take away the consideration of the Cathedral of Siena as one of the masterpieces of Italian Medieval Art.

The Exterior of the Cathedral

The *Façade* is completely in white marble with polychrome insertions of pink stone of Siena and green stone of Prato. As already mentioned, the lower section is in Romanesque style whilst the upper section is Gothic. The lower section is made up of three enormous arches topped with triangular spires. The central arch is round, whilst the two side arches are slightly pointed. The central portal is in bronze and was restored in

2

1958 by the sculptor *Enrico Manfini* and is decorated with images inspired by the life of Holy Mary. The sculptural section gives an elegant volumetric flow and is dedicated to the *Glorification of Our Lady of the Assumption, Her Advent* and to stories from the *Old Testament*. The statues that we see today are copies, as the originals, by *Giovanni Pisano* and his disciples, are kept in the *Museum of Metropolitan Art*. The architrave of the central portal has a bas-relief by *Tino di Camaino*, portraying stories of *St. Gioacchino and St. Anne*. To the sides there are strips of small columns decorated in classical style, the work of *Giovanni Pisano*. An enormous cornice that touches the tips of three spires erected over the portals separates the two sections of the façade. The Cathedral of Orvieto undoubtedly inspires the Gothic-Florentine style of the upper section by *Lorenzo Maitani*, where the three spires were internally decorated in mosaic by the Venetian *Augusto Castelleni* in 1877. The three mosaics depict: *The Coronation of Mary* in the centre; on the left the *Presentation at the Temple* and the *Holy Crib* on the right. The central rose window, placed under the large spire, is made up of a circular polychrome window depicting the *Last Supper* and is contained in a square marble cornice topped with a statue of the *Madonna*. In the four corners there are images of the Evangelists, whilst the sides contain the sculptured busts of *34 Prophets and Church Patriarchs*. The originals of these sculptures are also kept in the Museum of Metropolitan Art and the copies were made by *Leopoldo Maccari* last century. The great *Angel* at the top of the central spire is the work of *Tommaso Redi* in 1639. The church square in front of the three doors is composed of marble inlay, the work of *Nastagio di Gaspare* in the 15th century and depicting scenes of the *Ordination*. Two columns with the Senese she-wolf and the twins are situated on the sides of the square and are the work of Giovanni Pisano and Urbano da Cortona. These are also copies and the originals are kept in the Museum of Metropolitan Art.

On the **left hand side** a mullioned window with one light can only just be seen, as the entire side is incorporated into the adjacent *Palazzo Arcivescovile*.

1: *The right side with the entrance door to the bell-tower*
2: *The Dome and the Bell-tower; notice the elegance of the double rows of arches of the Dome*

1

The **right side** of the Cathedral is decorated on the lower part with horizontal strips in polychrome marble that alternate with black marble strips.

The upper section is finished in a lighter marble with Gothic tabernacle mullioned windows with two lights and the columns of the nave placed at intervals. Each of these columns holds up a statue of a *Prophet*.

In the central part of the cross vault, that appears to carry on from the side, there is a beautiful bronze portal by *Vico Consorti* (1946).

Over the portal there is a marble bas-relief depicting the *Madonna and Child* by *Donatello*, also known as the *Madonna of Forgiveness*.

The **bell tower** was built in 1313 on the pre-existing Romanesque style *Torre dei Bisdomini – Forteguerri* by *Agostino di Giovanni* and *Agnolo di Ventura*.

It is characteristic for its black and white horizontal strips that run along four sides from the bottom to the top.

The six windows, always on the four sides, rise from one light to six lights.

At the top there is a high pyramid with a hexagonal base, whilst the four corners have other pyramids with square bases.

The majestic **dome** is placed on a hexagonal based tambour with two orders covered in arcades surrounded by colonnades.

The lower arcade has acute arches supported by double columns, whilst the upper arcade has Roman arches.

2

The Interior of the Cathedral

Upon entering, the majestic grandeur of the Cathedral as a whole and the perfect matching of the polychrome marble colours that completely cover the walls and the columns are breathtaking.

The Cathedral is of an aisleless cruciform plan about ninety metres in length and twenty-four metres in width as far as the nave, the two aisles and the apse are concerned.

The two transepts measure fifteen metres each for a total of fifty-four metres of the two arms of the crucifix. By carefully observing the inside of the central portal, it is possible to see a slight asymmetry towards the right that corresponds with the presbytery.

This irregularity is due to the prolonging of the works and to the many restorations.

The nave and the two aisles are divided by polystyle columns that support Roman arches, whilst the vaulted roof is coloured dark blue with gold stars.

The walls and the columns are covered in black and white marble in horizontal strips in contrast to the vertical nature as a whole, making the entire area more suggestive.

An extremely long cornice sustained by the busts of *one-hundred and seventy-two Popes* runs along the two sides of the central nave and the presbytery, between the arches and the vaults, whilst a bust of Christ stands out in the apse.

The arches are decorated with large golden roses where the busts of *thirty-six Emperors* stand out.

1: The Cathedral: the central nave
2: A plan of the paving of the Cathedral

The Paving of the Floor

The paving of the Cathedral with its ornate decorations is without doubt one of the most interesting features of the temple.

It is made up of fifty-six marble inlay graffito panels produced at intervals starting from 1372 right through to 1562. The graffito panels are the oldest: this type of workmanship consisted in etching the design onto marble and then filling the incision with black stucco in order to make the designs stand out better. This is the most precious part of the floor and is normally covered: it is possi-

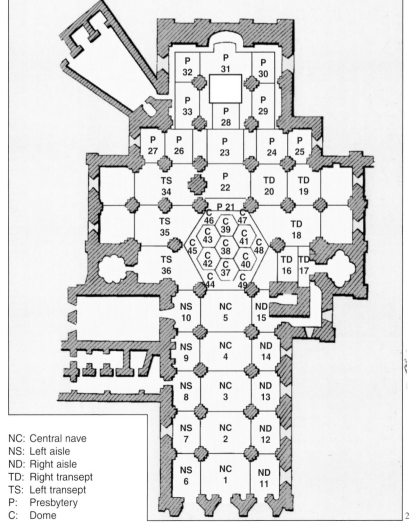

NC: Central nave
NS: Left aisle
ND: Right aisle
TD: Right transept
TS: Left transept
P: Presbytery
C: Dome

2

51

ble to view this section only from *August 15th to September 15th* every year. Subsequently, this workmanship was also carried out on dark marble with white stuccoing. The last panels were inlaid with different coloured marble.

The paving is the work of many artists such as *Domenico Beccafumi*, who created thirty-five panels between 1517 and 1547, *Domenico di Nicolò, Bastiano di Francesco, Matteo di Giovanni, Umberto da Cortona, Antonio Federighi* and *Pinturicchio*.

Not all the panels are original, as many of them were restored or substituted through time with identical copies. The plan on page 51 and the description that follows gives an accurate account of the paving:

Central Nave Paving
1. *Hermes Trismegisto*, by Giovanni di Stefano (1488)
2. *The Emblem of Siena* with the emblems of Pisa, Lucca, Florence, Arezzo, Orvieto, Rome, Perugia, Viterbo, Massa, Grosseto, Volterra and Pistoia
3. *Imperial Eagle* (1373)
4. *Fortune*, by Paolo Mannucci and designed by Pinturicchio (1504-06)
5. *Fortune and Four Philosophers*

Left Aisle Paving
6. *The Libyan Sybil*, by Guidoccio Cozzarelli (1483)

7. *The Hellespont Sybil*, by Neroccio di Bartolomeo Landi (1483)
8. *The Phrygia Sybil*, by Urbano da Cortona (1483)
9. *The Samia Sybil*, by Matteo di Giovanni (1483)
10. *The Albunea or Tivoli Sybil*, by Benvenuto di Giovanni (1483)

Right Aisle Paving
11. *The Delphi Sybil*, by Urbano da Cortona (1482)
12. *The Cumea Sybil*, by Urbano da Cortona (1482)
13. *The Cumana Sybil*, by Giovanni di Stefano (1482)
14. *The Eritrean Sybil*, by Antonio Federighi (1482)
15. *The Persian Sybil*, by Urbano da Cortona (1483)

Right Transept Paving
16. *The Seven Ages of Man*, by Antonio Federighi (1475)
17. *Faith, Hope, Charity and Religion*, by Domenico Beccafumi
18. *The Victory of Jephte over the Admonished*, by Bastiano di Francesco (1482)
19. *The Death of Absalom*, by Pietro di Minnella (1447)
20. *Emperor Sigismund on the Throne*, by Domenico di Bartolo (1434)

Presbytery Paving
21. *Moses causing Water to flow from the Rock*, by Domenico Beccafumi (1525)

22. *Adoration of the Golden Calf*, by Domenico Beccafumi (1522)

23. *David the Psalmist, David throwing the stone that hits Goliath*, by Domenico di Niccolò (1423)

24. *Moses*, by Paolo di Martino (1426)

25. *Samson's Victory over the Philistines*, by Paolo di Martino (1426)

26. *Joshua*, by Domenico di Niccolò (1426)

27. *The Victory of Joshua*, by Paolo di Martino (1426)

28 *The Sacrifice of Abraham*, by Domenico Beccafumi (1546)

29. *Prudence*, by Marchese d'Adamo (1380)

30. *Temperance*, by Marchese d'Adamo (1380)

31. *Mercy*, by Marchese d'Adamo (1406)

32. *Justice*, by Marchese d'Adamo (1406)

33. *Strength*, by Marchese d'Adamo (1406)

Left Transept Paving

34. *Judith decapitates Holofernes and the battle at the doors of Betullia*, by Antonio Federighi (1473)

35. *The Slaughter of the Innocents*, by Matteo di Giovanni (1481)

36. *Hercules Banished from the Throne*, by Benvenuto di Giovanni (1481)

Paving under the Dome

All of the following panels are by Domenico Beccafumi and were restored by Alessandro Franchi in 1870:

37. *Elias ascends to Heaven*

38. *The Pact between Elias and Ahab*

39. *The Sacrifice of Ahab*

40. *The Scolding of Elias*

41. *The Killing of the False Prophets*

42. *The Death of Ahab*

43. *The Sacrifice of Elias*

In the rhombuses around these panels we can see:

44. *Elias Resuscitates the Son of the Widow*

45. *Elias Anoints Jehu*

46. *Ardia conducts Ahab to Elias*

47. *Elias orders Ardia to take him to Ahab*

48. *The Deer nourishing Elias*

49. *Elias asks the Widow for bread*

1: *The emblem of Siena surrounded by emblems of allied cities*

2: *La Fortuna (n. 4 - central nave) by Paolo Mannucci, a design by Pinturicchio*

3: *Matteo di Giovanni, The Slaughter of the Innocents (n. 35 - left transept)*

3

The Internal Façade

At the pedestals of the columns of the central portal we can see bas-reliefs by *Urbano da Cortona* in 1483. They depict scenes of the *Story of Mary* and come from the ancient *Chapel of the Madonna delle Grazie*.

The columns are decorated by *Giovanni di Stefano* and come from the altar of the *Saints of the Crowned Four*.

There are beautiful 15th century bas-reliefs on the architrave that depict the stories of *St. Ansano*. The large rose window depicting *The Last Supper* is by *Pastorino dei Pastorini* (1549) on cardboard by *Perin del Vega*. Around the first two columns of the nave there are two beautiful holy water fonts by *Antonio Federighi* in 1463.

The Cathedral
1: Antonio Federighi: Holy Water Font

2: Pastorino De Pastorini: The Last Supper, a
stained glass window of the façade

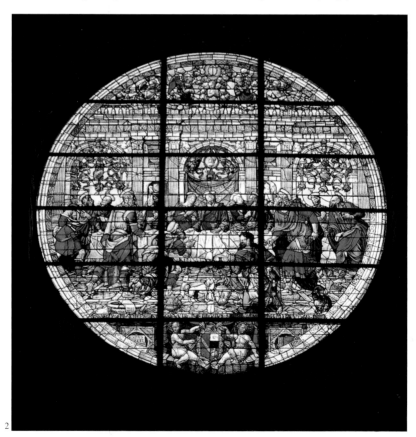

The Right Nave

Close to the internal façade, a statue of *Pope Pious V* by *Fulvio Signorini* (1605) can be found in a niche.

On the various altars there are many important works, such as:

on the 1st altar, *St. Gaetano* by Domenico Maria Canuti;

on the 2nd altar, *The Ecstasy of St. Girolamo* by Annibale Mazzuoli;

on the 3rd altar, *The Ecstasy of St. Francis Sales* by Raffaele Vanni;

on the 4th altar, *The Mystical Marriage of St. Catherine* by Pier Dandini.

At the end of the nave is the entrance door to the bell tower surrounded by six scenes of the *Life of Mary*, the work of Urbano da Cortona and on top, *The Tomb of Bishop Tommaso Piccolomini del Testa*, by Neroccio Bartolomeo Landi in 1485.

The Dome

The Dome has a hexagonal plan and is therefore held up by 6 pillars; the pillars that face the central nave have two Spars that originate from the Senese Carroccio that participated in the victorious battle of Montaperti.

Each corner of the pillars has a column that holds a golden statue of a saint.

The six statues are the work of *Ventura Tiparilli* and *Bastiano di Francesco*.

The large upper cornice, where there are 12 shell shaped niches, forms a closed arcade divided into 42 decorated columns.

The Dome is closed by a calotte with a lantern over the top that is very decentralised with respect to the axis of the pillars.

3: The Dome

The Right Transept

Like the left transept, this arm has a double nave divided by polystyle columns. On the right we can see the *Cappella della Madonna del Voto*, completed in 1661 by *Gian Lorenzo Bernini* upon the request of Pope Alexander VII, Fabio Chigi of Siena. It is in Baroque style with many decorations and a beautiful altar where there is a painting portraying the Madonna del Voto, work of the school of *Guido da Siena* in the 12th century. The bronze *Angels* that surround the painting are by *Bernini* as are the two marble statues of St. Girolamo and St. Mary Magda-lene that are placed on the sides of the entrance. Another two statues, of St. *Catherine and St. Bernard* are the works of *Ercole Ferrara and Antonio Raggi* and are placed in the niches of the altar. In continuing, we arrive at the *Cappella del Sacramento* (Chapel of the Sacrament), with its bas-reliefs on the walls that depict the *Evangelists and St. Paul*, the works of *Giovanni di Francesco* and *Giovanni di Turino*. On the altar is the work by *Alessandro Casolani* completed in 1594, *The Adoration of the Shepherds*.

The Chapel of the Madonna del Voto with its statues of St. Bernard, by Raggio and St. Catherine, by Ferrara

The Pesbytery

The beautiful *Altare Maggiore* is at the centre of the Presbytery, completely in marble and the work of *Baldasarre Peruzzi*.

On top is a large bronze *Tabernacle* by *Vecchietta* that comes from the Church of the Hospital of St. Maria della Scala and was brought here to substitute the *Maestà* by Duccio da Boninsegna, moved to the Museum of Metropolitan Art.

Up high we can see *2 Angel* candelabra holders, completed in 1489 by *Giovanni di Stefano*, whilst below there are another 2 Angels sculptured in 1498 by Francesco di Giorgio Martini.

Above the columns there are other 8 *Angels* in bronze that are the work of *Domenico Beccafumi* and date back to 1549. Up high again there are two *Choir Stalls* opposing each other; the one on the right is by *Antonio Barilli* (1511) and the one on the left is by *Riccio* (1550).

The Episcopal Seat is by Tito Corsini, designed by Riccio.

The Altare Maggiore with the bronze Tabernacle, by Vecchietta and the Angels Holding Candelabra, by Francesco di Giorgio Martini and Giovanni di Stefano.

The Apse

Domenico Beccafumi frescoed the upper part of the niche in 1544 and today, regardless of the restoration works, only Paradise and the Apostles can be seen. The lower part has a fresco of the *Assumption* by *Bartolomeo Cesi* (1594). On the sides there are two frescos by *Ventura Salimbeni* and they are: *Esther before Assuero* on the right and *The Hebrews in the Desert* on the left.

Along the whole length of the apse is a beautiful carved wooden choir stall, of which the central stalls were designed by *Riccio* and were completed by *Benedetto di Giovanni* between 1560 and 1570. The side stalls are much older and were built between 1363 and 1397 by *Giacomo del Tonghio*, whilst the beautiful inlaid mirrors are taken from the Monastery of St. Benedict outside Porta Tufi and are the work of *Friar Giovanni da Verona*.

The precious stained glass windows by *Duccio da Boninsegna* in 1288 are the oldest work of their kind in Italy. They portray *Death, the Assumption, The Coronation of the Virgin, the 4 Evangelists* and the *4 Patron Saints of Siena*.

The Chapter House

A beautiful, finely decorated portal opens to the left of the apse and through this portal we have access to the *Vestry*. From here, we cross a vestibule that houses a beautiful bronze bust of *Pope Alexander VII* by *Bernini* or the School of Bernini and arrive at the *Chapter House*. This House contains a collection of portraits of Senese Popes and Bishops. There are three very interesting tablets by Sano di Pietro: *The Preaching of St. Bernard in Piazza del Campo* (1430); *The Preaching of St. Bernard in Piazza S. Francesco* (1440); *Portrait of St. Bernard* (1470). It is interesting to note the 15th century architecture of the buildings in the first two tablets.

1: *The Cathedral: The Chapter House. Sano di Pietro, St. Bernard Preaching in the Piazza del Campo.*
2: *The Cathedral: Pulpit, by Nicola Pisano.*

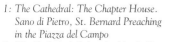

58

2

The Left Transept

Next to the pillars of the Dome it is possible to admire the splendid masterpiece by *Nicola Pisano*, *Pulpit*, sculptured between 1266 and 1269 with the help of his son Giovanni and Arnolfo di Cambio. It is quite similar to the Pulpit in the Baptistery at Pisa, the work of the same artist but completed a few years earlier. The Pulpit of the Cathedral of Siena is always in Gothic style, but with pre-Renaissance inspiration. It has on octagonal instead of hexagonal base, as has the work in Pisa. There are eight columns, four of which lean on lions and lionesses, whilst the central column presents the *8 Liberal Arts*: *Grammar, Dialectics, Rhetoric, Philosophy, Arithmetic, Geometry, Astronomy and Music.* At the top of the columns there are Corinthian capitals that support the stupendous and elegantly clover designed Triboli Arches. Two beautiful statutes

portraying the Virtues divide the arches. The parapet has seven bas-reliefs that are separated by images of Prophets and Angels, whilst the panels portray, beginning from the stairway: *Nativity and Visitation*, with the beautiful image of Mary; *the Arrival and Adoration of the Three Wise Men*; *Presentation at the Temple, St. Joseph's Dream and the Escape to Egypt; the Slaughter of the Innocents; Crucifixion; the Final Judgement of the Reprobates; the Final Judgement of the Good.*

The eighth space is the entrance to the Pulpit and access is via a beautiful staircase that is ornate with refined decorations and elegant columns.

Going back the same way to the right we can see the beautiful corner Chapel of St. Ansano. On the altar there is *St. Ansano Baptising the Senese*, a work by Francesco Vanni. On the left wall there is the *monument dedicated to Cardinal Riccardo Petroni*, by Tino da Camaino in

1318. Four caryatids support the sarcophagus. Over the sarcophagus is the figure of the Cardinal surrounded by four Angels with a Tabernacle depicting the Madonna and Child between St. Peter and St. Paul. The floor is made up of the bronze tomb stone of Bishop Giovanni Pecci, sculptured by Donatello in 1426.

Back to the transept we can see two beautiful statues: *Pope Pious II*, by Giuseppe Mazzuoli (1698) and *Pope Pious III*, by Piero Balestra (1706); whilst the floor has a graffito tombstone that dates to 1426.

We then move on to another two altars; the first has a beautiful canvas depicting the Madonna with St. Peter and St. Paul, by Salvatore Fontana. Instead, the second has a wooden Crucifix and statues of the Madonna, by Giovanni Evangelista and Maddalena.

We then cross a marble portal by Marrina and arrive at the Chapel of St. John the Baptist. The Renaissance style Chapel is the work of Giovanni di Stefano in 1482. The interior is richly decorated with stucco by Alberto Caponei and Cosimo Lucchi. On the left wall there is a canvas by Pinturicchio (1504) that depicts a young Alberto Aringhieri. Then there is a beautiful marble statue of *St. Ansano* by Giovanni di Stefano (1487) and a stupendous bronze statue of *St. John the Baptist* completed by Donatello in the final years of his life. Another canvas by Pinturicchio and finished by Rustichino portrays the *Decollation of St. John*, and a statue of *St. Catherine d'Alessandria* is the work of Neroccio di Bartolomeo (1487).

Other marvellous paintings by Pinturicchio portray: *an elderly Alberto Aringhieri; St. John the Baptist in the Desert; the Preaching of St. John; the Baptismal Font,* in the centre, is by Antonio Federighi.

The Cathedral - The Chapel of St. John the Baptist

The Left Aisle

At the fifth arch of the first sector there is the *Piccolomini Library*, built for the Cardinal Francesco Piccolomini, later to become Pope Pious III, to conserve the library of his uncle, Pope Pious II.

The entrance has two arches: in the right arch there is an altar with bas-reliefs that depict *St. John Evangelist* by Vecchietta, whilst the left arch has a beautiful Bronze Door by Ormanni (1497).

The lunette is decorated with a fresco by Pinturicchio in memory of the Corona-tion of Pope Pious II.

The interior, with its rectangular plan, is one of the most important Renaissance works.

The walls are divided by pilaster strips and are completely covered in frescoes by Pinturicchio depicting life scenes of Pope Pious II and that were completed between 1502 and 1509.

Starting from the window at the end on the right, the panels represent:

1 - A young Enea Silvio Piccolomini leaving for the Basilea Council
2 - Piccolomini is the Council's Ambas-sador for King James of Scotland
3 - Emperor Frederic III grants him his degree in poetry
4 - The invitation by Emperor Frederic III to become Ambassador for Pope Eugene IV
5 - As Bishop of Siena, Piccolomini pre-sents Eleonora of Portugal to her fiancé Frederic III at Porta Camollia
6 - Election as Cardinal by Pope Callis-tus III
7 - Election as Pontiff
8 - Proclamation of the Crusade against the Turks at the Congress of Mantua
9 - Pope Pious II canonises St. Catherine
10 - Pope Pious II goes to Ancona to solicit the departure of the Crusade.

The Piccolomini Chapel - The Three Graces

Under the frescos by Pinturicchio is an exhibition of beautifully ornate hymnbooks, the work of many artists such as Liberale da Verona, Girolamo da Cremona, Sano di Pietro, Pellegrino Mariano and Guidoccio Cozzarelli.

On a Renaissance style support in the centre of the Library there is the group of marble statues the *Three Graces*, a Roman copy of the sculpture of the Greek school of Prassitele, 3rd century BC. The centre of the ceiling has the emblem of the Piccolomini family surrounded by paintings with allegoric and mythological images. On top of the door there is a bas-relief, the work of *Jacopo della Quercia* that depicts the *Banishment of Adam and Even from Paradise on Earth*. The meiotic floor presents the emblems of the Piccolomini family.

Outside of the Library there is a group of sculptures that depicts *Christ Resurrected amongst the Angels*, by *Bandino Bandini*, a student of Michelangelo.

Moving further ahead, there is the stupendous *Piccolomini Altar*, a marble work by *Andrea Bregno* (1503).

The altar is in a large niche surrounded by other niches containing statues of *St. Gregory and St. Paul* to the right, whilst to the left the statues of *St. Peter and St. Pious*. These are early works of Michelangelo. In a higher niche there is the *Madonna* by *Jacopo della Quercia*.

The Cathedral - the Piccolomini Library
1: *Piccolomini Altar with statues of St. Paul, St. Gregory, St. Pious and St. Peter, sculptured by Michelangelo*
2: *Pinturicchio: Piccolomini in the robes of Bishop of Siena presents Eleonora of Portugal to Frederic III*
3: *Miniature Choir Stalls: Peter and Andrew abandon the nets to follow Christ*

7 - DUOMO NUOVO

The remains of what was to be the grandiose extension of the Cathedral is called the Duomo Nuovo. Work began in 1339 and was to occupy what is currently Piazza Jacopo della Quercia. All that remains of the Duomo Nuovo is the right aisle with 5 arches, whilst there are only 3 arches of the left aisle. The façade is striking in its grandeur and is aptly called Il Facciatone (the large façade), characterised by an enormous window divided into two parts.

The Cathedral - the Piccolomini Library
1: Pinturicchio: Emperor Frederic III grants
*   Piccolomini his degree in poetry*
Duomo Nuovo
2: Portal and stairway that leads to the
*   Baptistery*

8 - THE MUSEUM OF METROPOLITAN ART

Housed among the blind arches in the right hand aisle of the *Duomo Nuovo*, the museum was initiated in 1870 and has undergone continual renovation. All the most important original sculptures and paintings from the Cathedral are held here for their protection. The museum is divided into three sections.

The Ground Floor

Entering into a large room divided by a wrought iron gate which dates from the 15th century. Off to the left of the first section of the museum you can see a series of high-relieves from the 13th century depicting the *Annunciation*, *Christ's Birth*, *Flight to Egypt* and *Epiphany*. Also on the ground floor, a bas-relief, *St. Bernard* and a statue of St. Peter by Urbano da Cortona and a *Lion* by Giovanni Pisano are on show. In the second section of the museum the original statues of the two she-wolves that once stood on either side of the cathedral courtyard are on display. In the middle of the room there is a magnificent high-relief on which *Jacopo della Quercia's Madonna and Child*, *St. Girolamo and Cardinal Casini* are admirably sculpted. Note the beautiful paving on the floor and the 14th century tombstone of *Tommaso Pecci* which stands out among the paving stones. A long the walls the original ten statues which were sculpted by Giovanni Pisano between 1284 and 1296 originally used to decorate the façade of the cathedral can be admired and present a rare example of Gothic sculpture of this period. From left, the sculptures are: *Moses*, *Mary of Moses*, *Simeone*, *a Sybil*, *Isaiah*, *Balaam*, *David*, *Abacuc*, *Plato*, and *Solomon*.

There are also sculptures from the School of *Giovanni Pisano* amongst these statues. In the centre at the end, inserted into an altar, there is a large altarpiece painted in 1524 by *Brescianino* that depicts the *Baptism of Christ*.

The Museum of Metropolitan Art
1-2: Giovanni Pisano: Sculpture Room
3: Jacopo della Quercia: Madonna and Child,
*   St. Girolamo and Cardinal Casini*

1

The First Floor

To reach the first floor one has to go through the *Sala di Duccio* where what is considered to be the finest masterpiece by *Duccio da Boninsegna La Maestà* is held. It was painted between 1308 and 1311 on the altarpiece of the Altare Maggiore of the cathedral where it was until 1505. The great altar-piece made of wood which was painted on both sides was split in two, in 1771 so that it could be seen better. It is now safely stored in the museum where it has been since 1878.

In this masterpiece, the grand master transfused all his artistic sensitivity fusing the remnants of Byzantine art with the lyricism of emerging Senese-Gothic art. The *Madonna and Child on the throne among Angels, Saints Peter, John the Baptist, Agnes, Paul, John the Evangelist, Agatha and the four Patron Saints of the city, Ansano, Savino Crescenzio and Vittore* (Victor) are depicted in the foreground. Above, are the busts of the apostles. The back part on the walls in front, shows scenes from the Passion of Christ in a series of twenty-six pictures. The episodes are, from left to right and bottom to top: *The Entrance to Jerusalem; The Washing of the Feet; The Last Supper; The Conversation after Supper; Judas' Pact; Prayer in the Olive Grove; The Capture of Christ; Peter denies Jesus; Jesus in the presence of Anna; Jesus in the presence of Caifa; Jesus is beaten; Jesus at the Praetorium; Jesus sent away by Pilate; Jesus before Herod; The Scourging; The Crown of Thorns; The Climb to Calvary; Pilate washes his hands; The Crucifixion; The Deposition from the Cross; The Deposition into the Tomb; The devout women at the Tomb; The descent into Limbo; The apparition before Mary Magdalene; the apparition before Emmaus.*

The Museum of Metropolitan Art - Sala di Duccio da Boninsegna
1: La Maestà: front part
2: La Maestà: back part

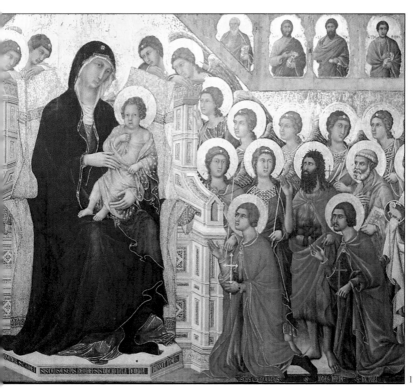

Before the altar-piece was split, the external border and the foot-pace were decorated with pictures, of which only 19 tablets remain in the museum, whilst the others can be found in other museums or have been lost.

In the same room it is possible to admire a magnificent triptych by *Pietro Lorenzetti* in 1342, the *Nativity of Mary* and a *Madonna and Child*, both early works of *Duccio da Boninsegna*.

Between the first and the second floors we can find the *Sala del Tesoro*, with its collection of church ornaments and works such as: *Reliquary of the head of St. Galgano*, a 13th century work of *Lando di Pietro*; *Reliquary of St. Clement*, of the 17th century; *Crown of St. Galgano*, of the 13th century; *Crucifix in golden wood*, by *Giovanni Pisano*.

We then arrive to the second floor and enter the *Sala of the Madonna with Big Eyes*. The name derives from the presence of a large 13th century painting by an unknown Senese artist that depicts the *Madonna and Child*, once on the Altare Maggiore of the Cathedral before being substituted with the *Maestà*. Vows were made to this Madonna on the eve of the battle of Montaperti.

In this room we can also find a polyptych by *Ambrogio Lorenzetti* with 4 Saints, *the Blessed Agostino Novello and His 4 mira-* cles, a masterpiece by *Simone Martini*, a *Madonna and Child* by *Sassetta*, and a *St. Paul* by *Domenico Beccafumi*.

In returning to the ground floor it is possible to visit the *Saloncino dei Conversari*, so called because of the readings held by *Vittorio Alfieri* in 1777.

After crossing another two rooms with their precious altar-frontals, we exit via a door on the right side of the Duomo Nuovo.

We proceed down a stairway designed by *Giovanni Sabatelli* in 1451 and called *Piaggia della Morte* (the descent of death) and find ourselves in the Crypt of the Cathedral.

The Museum of Metropolitan Art
   Sala di Duccio
1: *Pietro Lorenzetti: The Nativity of Mary*
   (detail) Room 2nd floor
2: *An anonymous Senese artist:*
   Madonna and Child, also called the
   Madonna with the Big Eyes

3: *The flight of steps known as the "Piaggia della Morte", half way up which you come to the crypt*
4: *The room where the statues of the apostles by artists from the School of Giovanni Pisano are shown*
5: *The Redeemer between two kneeling Angels by Govanni d'Agostino*

1

2

9 - THE CATHEDRAL CRYPT

The crypt was discovered while restoration work was being carried out. In it, were found various statues of the apostles by the artists from the School of Giovanni Pisano, copies of which can be seen adorning the cornice at the front of the Duomo Nuovo. Some precious fragments of frescoes which bear witness to the dawning of the School of Senese Painting which was founded in the 13th century can be admired here. Also of great artistic beauty is the marble statue representing the *Redeemer between two kneeling Angels*, which has been attributed to *Giovanni d'Agostino*. This sculpture, which has recently undergone restoration work, was

originally placed above the church door at the front of the Duomo Nuovo. The Baptistery in St. John's Square can be reached by going back down the stairs.

10 - THE BAPTISTERY

Also known as *Pieve di S. Giovanni* (Church of St. John), the Gothic style Baptistery was built between 1316 and 1325 and appears to be the design of *Domenico d'Agostino*.

The building leans against the apse of the Cathedral in an almost continuing way, seemingly the Crypt of the Cathedral and is completely finished in white marble.

The Façade

For reasons unknown, the upper part remains unfinished.

There are 3 magnificent portals of which only the central portal has a spire, whilst the two side portals have Roman arches.

Over the portals there is a beautiful cornice supported by small hanging arches with 3 slim closed pointed windows on top. The graffito paving of the church square depicts scenes relating to *Baptism and Confirmation*: to the left, *The Birth of the Child*, by *Bartolomeo di Mariano* (1450); in the centre, *The Child taken to the Baptistery* and the other images to the right are all works of *Antonio Federighi* and date back to 1451.

The Interior

The shape is rectangular and divided into 3 naves of two pillars that hold up the frescoed Gothic vaults, completed in 1325 by Camaino da Crescentino and *Tino da Camaino*.

The magnificent *Baptismal Font* is at the centre; it is a masterpiece by *Jacopo della Quercia* who designed this work in the first half of the 15th century combining elements of both Gothic and Renaissance styles, as the work was completed right in the years of transition from one style to the other.

It is set on 2 steps and the architectural component is the work of *Pietro del Minnella*, *Bastiano di Corso* and *Nanni di Lucca*, whilst the sculptural component was carried out by other artists.

The base is presented as a hexagonal basin with a column at the centre that supports the *Tabernacle*, also of hexagonal shape, with a statue of *St. John the Baptist* over it personally completed by *Jacopo della Quercia*.

The 6 sides of the basin are covered in golden bronze tiles, whilst the 6 corners are decorated with statues.

The façade of the Baptistery

With our backs to the Altar and proceeding towards the right, we can see: *The Angel Announces the Birth of Christ to Zachariah*, a tile by *Jacopo della Quercia*, 1417; *Justice*, a statue by Giovanni Turino, 1427; *The Birth of the Baptist*, tile by Turino di Sano, 1427; *Charity*, statue by Giovanni Turino, 1424; *The Preaching of the Baptist*, tile by Giovanni Turino, 1427; *Prudence*, statue by Giovanni Turino; *The Baptism of Jesus*, tile by Lorenzo Ghilberti, 1427; *Faith*, statue by Donatello; *The Capture of the Baptist*, tile by Lorenzo Ghilberti, 1427; *Hope*, statue by Donatello, 1428; *Herod's Banquet*, tile by Donatello, 1427; *Fortitude*, statue by Goro di Neroccio, 1428.

In the 6 niches of the Tabernacle we can see 5 statues of Prophets, each the work of Jacopo della Quercia, whilst the 6th niche holds a Madonna and Child by Giovanni Turino.

In the upper part of the Tabernacle, on the corners of the gables, there are 4 Angels, 2 by Donatello and the other 2 by Giovanni Turino in 1424.

The Baptismal Font by Jacopo della Quercia

The vaults towards the façade and the relative under arches were frescoed by *Vecchietta* in 1450 and portray *Apostles, Prophets and Sibyls*.

The other vaults depict the *Articles of the Creed*, frescos by disciples of Vecchietta, whilst attribution of the *Jesus in the House of the Pharisee* in the right lunette is dubious. The frescos of the apse represent *The Life of Jesus* and are the work of *Michele Matteo* for the upper section whilst the lower section is by *Vecchietta*.

The Baptistery, the Baptismal Font
1: *Hope, by Donatello*
2: *Herod's Banquet, by Donatello*
3: *The Baptism of Jesus, by Lorenzo Ghilberti*
4: *The Angel announces the Birth of Jesus to Zachariah, by Jacopo della Quercia*

73

11 - THE HOSPITAL OF SANTA MARIA DELLA SCALA

The Hospital stands opposite the steps of the Cathedral in a square named after it, and it is from its position in relation to these steps or "scala" as they are called in Italian, that the building gets its name. According to some historical sources the original nucleus of the building was built in the 9th century, however, the Hospital as we see it today was not built until the 13th cent. when the Cathedral Canons ordered its construction. The long façade is decorated in the centre by a facing of stone in which the two great portals are set, while the two outer wings and the upper storeys in which enormous mullioned windows with two lights are set, are covered with terracotta.

The Interior

You can admire a fine wooden ceiling in the first vestibule decorated by *Guidoccio d'Andrea* in the 15th century. On the left as you come in stands the *Tomb of Jacopo Tondi* executed by *Giacomo Cozzarelli*. In the second vestibule a beautifully painted fresco by *Domenico Beccafumi* (1512) depicts *The Meeting Between Saint Joachim and Saint Anne*. After crossing a room in which there are paintings of various saints you come the great Sala dell'infermeria (Infirmary) or Pellegrinaio, as it is also called, in which St. Catherine took care of the sick. This large hall is of even greater artistic importance because of a series of 15th century frescoes, the only ones of their kind, which illustrate in great detail the customs of that period and show people in the act of administering care to patients in need. The frescoes date from the 15th century and were executed by *Domenico di Bartolo* with the help of other artists, one of which was *Vecchietta*. By moving away from the main door, to the right you can see the following frescoes: Examples of Charity by *Domenico di Bartolo*, completed in 1440. Orphans being rescued and breasted, by *Domenico di Bartolo*; The wetnurses take care of the babies by *G. Novesi*, completed in 1507; The Wetnurses Salary by *Achille Crogi*; The Blessed Agostino Novello by *Pietro della Quercia*, 1432; The Hospital is Enlarged by *Domenico di Bartolo*, 1443; The Foundlings Ascend to Heav-

en by *Lorenzo Vecchietta*, 1441; Note on the vaults and on the arches the figures of the Patron Saints. The next ward is the Infirmary of St. Pious where fine frescoes by *Domenico di Bartolo*, consecrated to the Blessed, who is thought to be the founder of the hospital in the 9th century. Frescoes by *Vecchietta* and other artists are shown in the St. Peter's Room.

12 - THE CHURCH OF S. MARIA DELLA SCALA OR OF OUR LADY OF THE ANNUNCIATION

A short walk through the first vestibule of the hospital brings you to the Church of S.

Maria della Scala which was built in 1252 and restored in 1466 by *Guidoccio d'Andrea*. It is an aisleless church with a particularly interesting raised Presbytery and an exceptional lacunar ceiling. Also worthy of note are the two inlaid organs in front of the presbytery and the choir which is also inlaid and runs the full length of the apse wall. In the adjoining Cappella dei Malati (Chapel of the Sick) there are paintings which illustrate episodes from the life of the Virgin Mary while in the Oratory below there is another wooden choir which dates from the 15th century together with a beautiful marble Madonna on the altar. In the adjoining Oratorio della Confraternità dei Disciplinati (Oratory of the Brotherhood of The Disciplined) you will find other works of art well worth seeing, among which there are one or two exceptional pieces such as a Crucifix and two wooden statues, one of St. Catherine and the other of St. Bernard. The Sacristy holds a Pietà by *Sano di Pietro* and a Giudizio Finale (Last Judgement) by *Martino di Bartolomeo*.

To the left of the photograph, The Hospital of Santa Maria della Scala.
In the background, The Archbishop's Palace.
On the right, The Cathedral

13 - THE NATIONAL ARCHAEOLOGICAL MUSEUM

The Museum was established in 1956 in Via della Sapienza and then transferred here in 1988. The materials on exhibition are grouped into sections according to their places of origin.

The first section is a collection of finds that go from Palaeolithic to the Iron Age, plus Etruscan and Roman relics that date from the 7th century BC to the 3rd century AD.

In the other rooms there is the Topographical Section, where the finds are grouped according to the place in which they were found. The most important pieces come from the area around Chiusi. The Numismatic Section is also very interesting with its collection of Etruscan, Piceno, Umbro, Latium and Roman coins.

14 - PALAZZO ARCIVESCOVILE

The Archbishop's Palace leans against the right side of the Cathedral and in fact, almost covers it completely. It was built between 1718 and 1723 in an attempt to imitate the Gothic style of the Cathedral making the Piazza and its buildings more harmonious as a whole. The lower part of the façade is finished in white marble with longitudinal black strips. The arches of the door and the windows are also in black and white. The upper part is in cotto with two rows of mullioned windows with two lights.

Inside, kept in the *Chapel of St. Blaise*, is the beautiful spired painting depicting the *Madonna of Milk* by *Ambrogio Lorenzetti*.

15 - ST. SEBASTIAN IN VALLE PIATTA

Upon exiting the Palazzo Arcivescovile and going left, we arrive at a piazza where there is the St. Sebastian in Valle Piatta Church, assigned to the Oratory of the Contrada della Selva (Forest). Construction is in cotto by *Girolamo Ponsi* in the first half of the 16th century. The domed bell tower has a cylindrical cupola. The interior is of a Greek Cross plan, with precious decorations by 16th century Senese artists.

1: The National Archaeological Museum: Heavy Bucchero amphora (app. 4th cent. BC)
2: The Archbishop's Palace

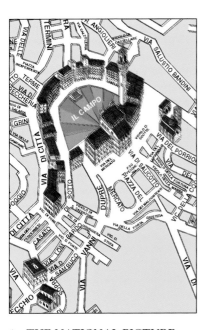

1 - THE NATIONAL PICTURE GALLERY

The National Picture Gallery is housed in the elegant late Gothic Palazzo Buonsignori with its marvellous terracotta façade in which Gothic doorways and mullioned windows with three lights are set. It is in this building that some of the finest examples of Senese art between the 12th and 17th centuries can be seen displayed in chronological order or in collections by a particular artist. The collection of canvasses was initiated towards the end of the 18th cent. by the Abbot *Giuseppe Ciaccheri*, and was then continued with the contribution of donations from various Convents, Churches and Brotherhoods that were suppressed. When in 1930, the collection became the property of the State it was moved into the present location of the Institute of Fine Arts, where it had originally been stored. Here, over 700 paintings are on show in the building's 38 rooms. In the hall there are some works of art which date back to the Roman period, while in the colonnade outside in the courtyard, which you can reach through a beautiful marble doorway, there are some coats of arms, bas-relief work and various Medieval sculptures on show. The Picture Gallery is on the first floor on which there are various rooms that contain such a large number of masterpieces that we can only give a brief description of those works considered to be the most important in the space available to us. A more thorough analysis would require more space.

Palazzo Buonsignori

All the works of art have the title, the name of the artist, the date the painting was executed and other helpful pieces of information which give a good idea of the different artistic tendencies in their historical contexts.

Room I: a beautiful rare painting on linen canvas that depicts *The Transfiguration, Jesus' Entrance to Jerusalem, The Resurrection of Lazarus*, all works by *Guido da Siena*.

Room II: a painting with *St. Peter Seated on the Throne* and 6 *Sacred Stories* on the sides, and early work of *Guido da Siena*.

Room III: a magnificent polyptych, the work of *Duccio da Boninsegna* and of his School, depicting a *Madonna and Child and the Saints Agnes, John the Baptist, John Evangelist and Magdalene*.

Room IV: here we find the famous *Madonna of the Franciscan Order* by *Duccio da Boninsegna*, painted around 1300 with a refined miniaturist technique.

1

Rooms V and VI: here there are several painting masterpieces by *Simone Martini*, such as a *Madonna and Child*, a *Madonna of Mercy* and a *Blessed Agostino Novello and his Miracles*.

Room VII: in this room there is a collection of several masterpieces by *Ambrogio Lorenzetti*. A triptych of the first half of the 14th century portrays a *Madonna and Child, St Mary Magdalene and St. Dorothy*. There are also two tablets of *A City by the Sea* and *A Castle on the Lake* that are extremely famous as they have a landscape as their subject, the first of their kind in Europe.

In this room there is also a *Madonna and Child, Saints, Church Doctors and Angels*, also known as the *Piccola Maestà*; an *Annunciation* dated 1344 by the Artist and famous for its interesting perspective.

The National Picture Gallery
1: <u>Room IV</u>: *The Madonna of the Franciscan Order, by Duccio da Boninsegna*
2: <u>Room V</u>: *Madonna and Child, by Simone Martini*

2

Room VIII: two masterpieces by *Bartolo di Fredi* of the second half of the 14th century: *The Adoration of the Three Wise Men, Scenes of the Life of the Virgin.*

Room IX: a triptych by *Bernardo Daddi* of 1336 portrays a *Madonna and Child, the Nativity and Crucifixion.*

Room X: here there is a 14th century painting by a Bolognaise artist with the *Saints Cosma and Damian.*

Room XI: in this room there is a collection of works by *Taddeo di Bartolo* such as the triptych of 1409 with *The Adoration of the Shepherds, Annunciation and Saints.*

Room XII: a collection of works by *Giovanni di Paolo*: *The Altar-piece of Staggia, the Piccola Maestà, St. Andrew Apostle.*

Room XIII: *The Last Supper* and *St. Anthony Abbot beaten by the Devils*, by Sassetta.
There are also two paintings by Giovanni di Paolo of 1445 - the *Madonna of Humility, Patient Christ and Triumphant Christ.*

Room XIV: *Potiphar's Wife and Chaste Joseph*, *Susanna at the baths* and *Joseph sold by his brothers* are three tablets by Francesco di Giorgio Martini. There is also the masterpiece by *Neroccio di Bartolomeo*, *Madonna and Child and Saints Girolamo and Bernardino* (1475).

Room XV: *The Adoration of the Shepherds with Saints Galgano and Martin*, the only work by *Pietro di Domenico.*

Room XVI: here there is a collection of works by *Sano di Pietro* such as: *the Assumption of the Madonna*, a painting; *Madonna and Child and 8 Angels*; *St. Girolamo in the Desert.*

The National Picture Gallery

1: <u>Room VII:</u> *The Nativity of the Virgin and four Saints, by Paolo di Giovanni Fei*

2: <u>Room XVII:</u> *Some works by Sano di Pietro*

3: <u>Room XIX:</u> *Panel of the "arliquiera", or the wardrobe of relics, by Lorenzo di Pietro (Vecchietta)*

4: <u>Room XXIII:</u> *The Holy Family and St. John, by Pinturicchio*

Room XVII: also in this room there are works by *Sano di Pietro*, such as the triptych *the Coronation of the Virgin amongst 4 Saints*, and another triptych *Madonna and Child, St. Girolamo, the Blessed Giovanni Colombini and Saints Cosma and Damian*.

Room XVIII: *Madonna and Child and Angels* by *Domenico di Bartolo*, 1433.

Room XIX: *The Coronation of the Virgin* by Francesco di Giorgio Martini. *St. Bernard* by *Vecchietta*.

Room XX: *Madonna and Child and Saints* by *Andrea di Niccolò*.
The Annunciation, miniature paintings by *Girolamo da Cremona*.

Room XXIII: *The Holy Family with St. John* by *Pinturicchio*.

Room XXIV: *The Martyrdom of St. Martina*, by *Pietro da Cortona*. *St. George amongst Faith and Charity*, by *Ventura Salimbeni*.

Room XXV: *the Martyrdom of St. Ansano* and the *Miracle of St. Eligio*, works by *Rutilio Manetti*.

Rooms XXVI, XXVII, XXVIII, XXIX and XXX are under rearrangement, however it is possible to admire *The Nativity*, by *Sodoma* (1503).

Room XXXI: *Judith* and *Christ at the Pillar*, two works by *Sodoma*. *The Stigmata of St. Catherine*, an early masterpiece by *Domenico Beccafumi*.

Room XXXII: *The Deposition of the Cross*, a magnificent painting by *Sodoma*.

Rooms XXXIII, XXXIV, XXXV and XXXVI are used for temporary exhibitions. When there are no exhibitions, cardboard sketches by *Domenico Beccafumi* for the paving of the Cathedral are exhibited.

Room XXXVII: *The descent of Christ into Limbo* and the *Prayer in the Garden*, by *Sodoma*. *The Annunciation* is a golden wood sculpture by *Jacopo della Quercia*.

2 - THE HOUSE
OF PIA DEI TOLOMEI

Upon exiting the National Picture Gallery, to our right we can see an elegant Gothic style building. This building is famous for housing the woman who *Dante* made immortal in his *Divine Comedy*. The woman was the widow of Baldo Tolomei, remarried to Nello Panocchieschi and who, accused of adultery, spent the rest of her days in an isolated manor in Maremma.

3 - THE CHURCH
OF ST. PETER ALLE SCALE

Also known as the Church of St. Peter in Castelvecchio, we reach this church after having climbed a long stairway. The building was originally built in the 1200's, but completely restructured in the 18th century. The interior has a single nave and it is possible to admire *Our Lady of the Assumption*, by *Rustichino*; *Escape to Egypt*, by *Rutilio Manetti*; *S. Lucy with the Archangel Gabriel*, by *Sano di Pietro*; 4 Saints, canvasses by *Ambrogio Lorenzetti*.

1: *Porta S. Marco*
2: *The Church of St. Peter alle Scale*
3: *Via S. Pietro*
4: *St. Joseph's Arch*
5: *Piazza del Mercato: in the centre, the Loggia of Palazzo Pubblico*

4 - THE CHURCH OF ST. AUGUSTINE'S

The earliest part of the building was completed in the 13th cent., however over time it has been subjected to various changes and modifications. The last restoration work which transformed both the façade of the church and its interior, was completed in 1755 by the architect Luigi Vanvitelli. The façade is, in part, hidden by a porch which connects it to the adjacent old convent, now the headquarters of the National Tolomei Boarding School. It is an aisleless cruciform church, having one central nave in which many works of art are held. For example, there is a magnificent altarpiece of the Crucifix and Saints executed by *Perugino* in 1506 situated on the second alter to the right. The Chapel Piccolomini, to the right of the transept also holds such treasures as The Blessed Saint Augustine Novello and Scenes from his life, a splendid altar-piece by *Simone Martini* (1330) on the right hand wall, *L'Epifania* (Epiphany) another masterpiece by Sodoma, which you can see at the attar, *Madonna seated on a Throne*, a splendid fresco by Ambrogio Lorenzetti situated on the lunette in front of the altar, and the splendid The Slaughter of the Innocent painted on the left hand wall by *Matteo di Giovanni* in 1482. Leaving the nave you find yourself in the Presbytery surrounded by four Chapels in which you can admire the meiotic floors, a polychrome marble Tabernacle and an Urn containing the relics of the Blessed St. Augustine Novello. A long the left wall of the nave, positioned at the third altar, a Battesimo di Costantino catches the eye. It is the work of *Francesco Vanni* and dates from 1586. The second altar-piece on the same side shows the work of *Carlo Maratta*, Immaculate Conception.

St. Augustine's Church
1: Epiphany by Sodoma
2: Enthroned Madonna by Ambrogio Lorenzetti
3: The church complex

5 - THE CHURCH OF ST. PETER AND ST. PAUL

The church was built in the 17th century by *Flaminio del Turco*.

A portico precedes the façade and the interior has a Greek Cross plan, decorated with magnificent stuccoes.

On the right Altar there is a beautiful *Madonna of the Rosary* of the 13th century. The Altare Maggiore has the *Coronation of the Virgin* by *Andrea del Brescianino*. On the left Altar, *The Conversion of St. Paul* by *Astolfo Petrazzi*.

1: *The fountain of the Contrada dell'Onda (Wave)*
2: *The fountain of the Contrada della Torre (Tower)*
3: *The lawn of St. Augustine and St. Joseph's Church*

6 - THE CHURCH OF ST. NICCOLO' DEL CARMINE

Apart from the Church, the complex also comprises of a bell tower with 4 orders and a Cloister richly adorned with frescos. The Church was built in the 14th century, but was partially transformed in the 16th century by *Baldassarre Peruzzi*.

The interior was left almost entirely intact: it has only one nave and a trussed ceiling with paintings.

The Church houses many works of art: **in the right side** we can find *the Adoration of the Shepherds*, a work begun by *Duccio da Boninsegna* and completed by *Arcangelo Salimbeni*.

On the 1st Altar, the *Assumption of Mary*, part of a fresco by *Gualtiero di Giovanni*.

On the 2nd Altar, *St. Michael*, by *Domenico Beccafumi*.

After the 2nd Altar, the remains of a fresco, *The Annunciation*, by *Ambrogio Lorenzetti*.

In the Chapel of the Sacrament there is a beautiful Altar by *Lorenzo Marrina* with two masterpieces by Sodoma: *The Nativity of Mary* and *The Eternal Father*. Also worth mentioning is the *Madonna of Mantellini*, a painting of the Senese School that dates back to 1240.

In the Presbytery there is the beautiful marble Tabernacle placed over the Altare Maggiore.

In the apse there is a Byzantine style painting of the *Madonna del Carmine*.

On the left side at the 3rd Altar there is the *Martyrdom of St. Bartholomew* by *Alessandro Casolani*, whilst at the 2nd Altar there is the *Ascension of Jesus* by *Girolamo del Pacchia*.

7 - THE ORATORY OF ST. ANSANO

The Oratory was built in the 9th century and restored during the 15th century. For a certain period it was assigned to the Chapel of the St. Ansano Gaol and is believed to have been the first Baptistery of the city.

In front of the cotto façade of the Oratory rises the *Torre della Rocchetta*, perhaps of Roman origin and completely in stone.

1: The Church of St. Niccolò del Carmine

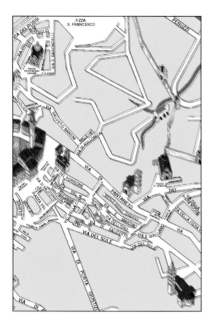

1 - FONTE DI FOLLONICA

The Fonte di Follonica was built in the 13th century and was completely restored during the current century. It has 3 large pointed arches and is certainly one of the most beautiful of the famous Senese fonts.

2 - THE CHURCH OF THE HOLY SPIRIT

This Renaissance style church was built in the final years of the 15th century. It has a simple, cotto façade and is adorned with a beautiful marble portal by *Baldassare Peruzzi* (1519).

In the square in front of church there is the beautiful *Fontana dei Pispini* built in 1534.

The dome is by *Giacomo Cozzarelli*. The aisleless, cruciform interior has only one nave and a very deep presbytery.

On the right wall there is a beautiful terracotta coloured Holy Crib behind iron bars, the work of *Ambrogio delle Robbia* in 1504. We then find the *Cappella of the Spagnoli*, which houses magnificent canvasses and frescos by *Sodoma* that represent: *St. Anthony Abbot*, a fresco on the right wall; *St.*

Sebastian, a fresco on the left wall; *St. Giacomo da Campostela*, a fresco on the ceiling; *St. Nicola da Tolentino and St. Michael Archangel*, canvasses placed over the Altar.

The Apse: on the 4 pillars of the Altare Maggiore there are 4 statues by *Rutilio Manetti* in 1608, whilst the walls boast a beautiful fresco by *Giuseppe Nasini, The Pentecost*. There are also 2 beautiful *Choir Stalls*.

The Left Wall: in the 3rd Cappella there is a beautiful wooden Crucifix, the work of *Sano di Pietro* and two wooden statues that depict *St. Girolamo* and *La Madonna*, the work of *Giacomo Cozzarelli*.

In the 2nd Cappella, a wooden statue of *St. Catherine of Siena* by *Cozzarelli*.

In the 1st Cappella, on the Altar, *Our Lady of the Assumption* and *Saints Francis and Catherine*, a 16th century work by *Andrea Balducci*.

1: Porta Romana - the apse and the Cloister of St. Mary of the Servants above
2: St. Mary of the servants: the façade and the bell tower

3 - THE CHURCH OF ST. MARY OF THE SERVANTS

A long stairway in Piazza A. Manzoni brings you to the Church at the top which was built in the 13th cent.. It underwent restoration work, however, over the following two hundred years. The façade has only one main door and two large roses. The bell-tower is of the same period but was recently restored, and has four windows on each side which gradually enlarge as they go up the tower as mullioned windows with one light give way to mullioned windows with four lights. The cruciform interior is composed of a nave and two aisles divided by Roman arches supported by marble columns. The nave reflects the characteristic Renaissance style while the transept and apse show Gothic style.

The works housed in the Church of St. Mary of the Servants are:

The entrance: a holy water font of 1200 and a Crucifix that dates to 1300.

The right aisle: at the 1st Altar outside the Cappella, the remains of frescos of 1300.

At the 2nd Altar, *The Madonna of Bordone*, a Byzantine style work of the 1300's by *Coppo di Marcovaldo*.

At the 3rd Altar, *The Nativity of the Virgin*, by *Rutilio Manetti*.

At the 5th Altar, *The Slaughter of the Innocents* and *Madonna and Saints*, 15th century works by *Matteo di Giovanni*.

The Presbytery: in the 2nd Cappella to the right, *The Slaughter of the Innocents*, a fresco by *Pietro Lorenzetti* and on the Altar, *The Madonna of the People*, by *Lippo Lemmi*.

On the Altare Maggiore, *The Coronation of Mary*, a magnificent altar-piece by *Bernardino Fungai*.

In the 2nd Cappella to the left, *Herod's Banquet* and *The Death of St. John Evangelist*, 2 frescos by *Pietro Lorenzetti*.

The left aisle: at the 2nd Altar, *The Madonna of Belvedere*, by *Mino del Pelicciaio* (1363) and at the sides, *The Coronation of the Virgin* and *St. Joseph*, 2 works by *Bernardino Fungai*.

At the 1st Altar, *The Annunciation* by *Francesco Vanni*.

Upon exiting the church, it is possible to visit the *Oratory of Holy Trinity* between the left transept and the apse. It was built at the end of the 13th century and restored in the 16th century. The interior is richly adorned with stuccoes and

has beautiful frescos by *Raffaele Nanni* and *Giuseppe Nasini* on the walls. Ventura Salimbeni frescoed the vault and the lunette. In the right Chapel there is a canvas by *Sano di Pietro* of the *Madonna and Child*. In the Vestry there is also a *Madonna and Child* and *John the Baptist* by Neroccio di Bartolomeo.

St. Mary of the Servants
1: *Madonna and Child,*
   by Coppo di Marcovaldo
2: *The interior of the church*
3: *The Slaughter of the Innocents,*
   by Pietro Lorenzetti
4: *The Coronation of Mary,*
   by Bernardino Fungai

4 - ST. GIROLAMO'S CHURCH

Situated in the street of the same name, we reach this church after having walked through a labyrinth of narrow streets that made up the *Jewish Ghetto* and having passed the *Oratory of St. Giacomo*, which houses a collection of works by *Sodoma*.

It is an aisleless church that was built in the 14th century.

Inside, to the right between the 2 Altars is the *Tombstone of Bishop Bettini*, a work by *Giacomo Cozzarelli* that dates back to 1507.

In the left Cappella, *The Coronation of Mary* by *Sano di Pietro* (1465).

In the annexed Convent, the Cloister is decorated with frescos by *Bernardino Fungai*.

5 - ST. GEORGE'S CHURCH

This church was built at the end of the 13th century in memory of the victory at the battle of Montaperti but underwent restoration works in 1741 at the hands of *Giovanni da Cremona*, who restored the façade in Baroque style.

The Romanesque bell tower remains the original, and inside there is the tomb of Francesco Vanni.

6 - THE CHURCH OF ST. JOHN THE BAPTIST DELLA STAFFA

Walking down Via del Pantaneto, on the right in Piazza S. Giovannino, there is this beautiful 13th century church that underwent restoration works in the 16th and the 19th centuries. Inside we can find a collection of works by famous artists such as *Ventura Salimbeni, Rutilio Manetti, Raffaele Vanni, Antonio Federighi and Paolo di Giovanni di Fei*. In walking back up the medieval Via Bandini, it is possible to visit the Corte del Castellare degli Ugurgieri, a building that has been entirely preserved, even in the smallest detail, in its medieval characteristics.

7 - ARCHCONFRATERNITY OF MERCY

The Archconfraternity was founded in the 13th century by the *Blessed Andrea Gallerani* for the care of the sick and the needy. The building comprises an Oratory that houses 2 wooden statues by *Lorenzo Murrina*, an Our Lady of the Assumption and a Gabriel.

In the Sala del Consiglio (Meeting Room) there are works by *Beccafumi* and *Cozzarelli*.

A nocturnal view

8 - ST. MARTIN'S CHURCH

This church was built in 1537 and designed by *Giovanni Battista Pelori*, however Giovanni Fontana completed the façade only in 1613. It has an aisleless cruciform interior with only one nave and a large central dome with frescos by *Annibale Mazzuoli*.

It houses a collection of many works, such as:

The right wall: at the 2nd Altar, *Circumcision*, a work by *Guido Reni* in 1640; at the 3rd Altar, *the Martyrdom of St. Bartholomew* by *Guercino* with a beautiful marble cornice by *Lorenzo Murrina*. In front of the Altare Maggiore there are 5 golden wooden statues that depict: *Madonna and Child*, by *Jacopo della Quercia*, and *Saints Peter, Bartholomew, John and Anthony Abbot*, all works by della Quercia's disciples.

These statues were sculptured between 1419 and 1425.

The right transept: here there is a beautiful statue of *St. Thomas of Villanova* by *Giovanni Mazzuoli*, whilst on the Altar there is *The Conception* by Mazzuoli's brother, *Giuseppe*.

The Altare Maggiore is the work of *Lorenzo Murrina*, whilst the statues are by *Giuseppe Mazzuoli*.

The apse: here there is a beautiful stained glass window depicting *St. Martin* by *Pastorino dei Pastorini*.

The left wall: on the 3rd Altar by Murrina, *The Nativity* by *Domenico Beccafumi*. On the 2nd Altar there is a group of wooden statues of the 15th century, with Crucifix between the Madonna and St. John Evangelist.

On the 1st Altar, *St. Ivone* by *Raffaele Vanni*.

9 - THE LOGGIA OF THE POPE

The loggia are situated in Via Banchi di Sotto and were erected in 1462 by *Antonio Federighi* on instruction of Pope Pious II, who, in an effort to make Siena more beautiful and important, wanted to create a meeting place for his family and their friends. The Renaissance style building has 3 large stone arches leaning against Corinthian columns. The internal decorations are by *Francesco di Giorgio Martini*.

10 - ST. VIGIL'S CHURCH

This church has been the home of the Camaldolites, the Jesuits and the Vallombrosian orders, therefore has undergone many transformations.
The façade is of the 18th century by *Antonio Meucci*. The single nave interior has a coffered ceiling painted by *Raffaele Vanni* in Baroque style. On the various altars of the walls of the nave there are works by *Mattia Preti* and *Volterrano*.

11 - PALAZZO OF THE UNIVERSITY

The Palazzo was once the Convent of the adjacent St. Vigil's Church. It has housed the University since 1814, but when it was built in the 13th century it was occupied by the *Studio Senese*, one of the oldest in Italy. It has a beautiful courtyard surrounded by porticoes elegantly decorated with stuccoes and frescos.

The Palazzo of the University
The frescoed ceilings of the portico

12 - ST. CHRISTOPHER'S CHURCH

This church is situated in Piazza Tolomei in front of the Palazzo of the same name. Originally built in the Romanesque era, it was completely restored in 1720.

The church was the meeting place of the *Consiglio of the Repubblica* (The Council of the Republic) before the Palazzo Pubblico was built.

The cotto façade has 4 columns and 2 statues.

The single nave interior contains many works of art, such as: *St. Christopher and St. George Killing the Dragon*, an altar-piece by *Sano di Pietro* and a 14th century wooden Crucifix covered in leather.

13 - PALAZZO TOLOMEI

This building faces onto the piazza of the same name where a column rises with a tin Senese she-wolf on top. It was built in Gothic style with a large door and 2 rows of Gothic arch mullioned windows with two lights.

Construction works began in 1205, therefore this solid stone building is one of the oldest in the city.

Via S. Caterina

14 - THE CHURCH OF ST. PETER IN OVILE

Of the original Romanesque style building that dates back to the 13th century, only the façade remains. The rest of the building was completely transformed during the 18th century.

The interior has a nave and two aisles and houses a collection of many works of art, such as: on the right Altar, an imitation of *The Annunciation* by *Simone Martini*, the work of *Matteo di Giovanni*. In the apse there is a beautiful Crucifix by *Giovanni di Paolo*.

On the altar left of the Altare Maggiore, we can admire a *Madonna* and *St. John Evangelist*, 2 beautiful wooden statues by Domenico di Niccolò dei Cori (1415).

On the left Altar, *Madonna and Child*, by the *Maestro of St. Peter in Ovile*.

15 - THE CHURCH OF ST. MARIA OF PROVENZANO

This holy building was designed and constructed by *Flaminio del Turco* in 1594. The façade is in white stone and has 4 pillars that divide it vertically. On top there are 2 large cornices that close in 3 windows.

The large and slender dome rises over and octagonal base tambour. The Baroque style interior is aisleless and cruciform with a single nave. The church houses a collection of famous works of art, such as, from the **right wall**, at the 1st Altar, St. Cerbone by *Rutilio Manetti* (1630) and moving along to the pillars of the dome we can find trophies stolen from the Turks.

In the **right transept** there is the *Vision of St. Catherine* by *Francesco Rustici*. On the Altare Maggiore, *The Madonna of Provenzano*, a 13th century work protected by a magnificent Tabernacle.

In the **left transept**, *St. Mary Magdalene* and *St. John Evangelist*, two statues placed on the sides of a beautiful Crucifix, are both works of the 17th century.

The Vestry: *Madonna*, a 14th century Senese School fresco; *The Holy Family* by *Francesco Vanni*; *The Pietà*, by *Cristoforo Casolani*. The Church holds the Palio of the Contrade, held on July 2nd of every year, in memory of the Miracles of the Madonna.

16 - ST. FRANCIS' BASILICA

A short walk along evocative streets flanked by Medieval buildings and St. Francis' Arch brings you out into the square in front of the Basilica. The construction of the Basilica in Gothic style was begun in 1326 on the site of an older church, but was only finished a cent. later in 1475. The original project for the building was drafted by *Agostino di Agnolo* however, *Francesco di Giorgio Martini* finished off the work. After being badly damaged by fire in 1665, it was rebuilt in Baroque style. However, at the turn of the cent., a project by Giuseppe Partini was drawn up to restore the Basilica to its original state and the task of rebuilding the façade was delegated to Vittorio Mariani and Gaetano Ceccarelli. The interior follows an Egyptian cross plan and has one large nave with horizontal black and white stripes decorating the walls with a trussed roof made of unpainted wood. Note the beautiful stained-glass, mullioned windows with two lights that embellish the walls and in particular, the mullioned window with four lights in the apse.

Here too, you will find many interesting works of art.

1: *The Church of St. Maria of Provenzano*
2: *St. Francis' Basilica: below to the right, the Church of St. Maria of Provenzano*

Here too you will find many works of art, such as:

On **the right wall**, in the first lunette and the niche that follows, *Visitation* and *The Saints*, 2 frescos of the Senese School of the 14th century; immediately after the side entrance, *The Tomb of Pia dei Tolomei*.

The right transept: *St. Francis*, a beautiful statue by *Francesco di Valdambrino*, can be found on a column in the corner. In the 2nd Cappella there is the *Tomb of Cristoforo Felici* by *Urbano da Cortona* (1462). In the 1st Cappella there is a *Madonna and Child* By Andrea Vanni.

The Presbytery: a beautiful stained glass window by *Zatter di Monaco*. There are also two portraits of the parents of Pope Pious II on the left wall that date back to the 16th century and represent what remains of the *Tomb of the Piccolomini Family*.

The left transept: in the 1st Chapel, *Crucifixion*, and a beautiful 14th century fresco by *Pietro Lorenzetti*. In the 2nd Chapel, to the right, *St. Ludovic before Boniface VIII* and to the left, *the Martyrdom of 6 Franciscan Monks at Ceuta*, frescos by *Ambrogio Lorenzetti*.

The left wall: in the 6th Chapel, the so-called Chapel of the Sacrament, there is an important graffito floor by *Lorenzo Murrina*.

We enter the Cloister by going through a door with a Renaissance style arcade and a portal. This is the ancient passageway to the ex St. Francis' Convent that today houses the Regional Seminary Pious II.

St. Francis' Basilica
1: The interior
2: St. Ludovic before Boniface VIII,
*   by Ambrogio Lorenzetti*
3: The Martyrdom of Six Franciscan Monks,
*   by Ambrogio Lorenzetti*

17 - THE ORATORY OF ST. BERNARD

The Oratory lies slightly to the right of St. Francis' Basilica and was built in the 15th cent. on the spot where Saint Bernard used to preach.

The building is made up of two oratories, one on top of the other which contain some very valuable masterpieces.

The Lower Oratory: holds a fine Madonna and Child with Saints, by Brescianino. There are also two beautiful statues in painted terracotta of St. Bernard and St. Catherine.

In the first vestibule on the first floor there is a fine wooden statue carved by members of the School of *Jacopo della Quercia* while the altarpiece shows a Madonna by Sano di Pietro and to the left a bas-relief by *Giovanni d'Agostino*.

The Upper Oratory: has a remarkable lacunar ceiling which was decorated by Ventura Turapilli in the 15th cent.. The walls divided by slim pilasters decorated in stucco-work show a series of splendid frescoes which run from the left hand corner of the wall directly opposite the main entrance.

They are: St. Ludovic by *Sodoma*, The Nativity of Mary by *Girolamo del Pacchia*, The Presentation of Mary at the Temple, by *Sodoma*, The Wedding, by *Domenico Beccafumi*, St. Bernard by *Girolamo del Pacchia*, The Archangel Gabriel also by del *Pacchia*, The Glory of the Madonna and Saints, by *Domenico Beccafumi*, The Annunciation, by *Girolamo del Pacchia*, St. Anthony of Padua, by *Sodoma*, The Visitation by *Sodoma*, Mary's Journey by *Domenico Beccafumi*, The Annunciation, by *Sodoma*, St. Francis of Assisi, by *Sodoma*, The Coronation of Mary, by *Sodoma*.

The Oratory of St. Bernard
1: The Upper Oratory
2: The Nativity of Mary,
   by Girolamo del Pacchia
3: The Presentation of Mary at the Temple,
   by Sodoma

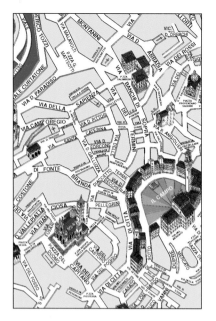

1 - ST. DOMINIC'S BASILICA

We begin this itinerary of the northern part of the city at the majestic St. Dominic's Basilica that is situated in the piazza of the same name. Work on the construction of the building commissioned by the Order of Dominican Monks, was begun in 1225 in Gothic style but was not completed for various reasons until 1465. During this time lapse the crypt was built, often called the Chiesa di Sotto or the Underground Church. It is most impressive when seen the side that drops sheer to the valley below where the *Fonte Branda* lies. In 1532 damage caused by fire was repaired contributing to the number of other architectural interventions that have changed the outside appearance of the building, which has only recently been restored to its original state. The severe façade in terracotta is flanked to the left by a towering belfry built in 1340. It was later lowered and crowned with merlons in the 18th cent.. The Church follows an Egyptian cruciform design and has only one large nave with a trussed wooden ceiling.

The Chapel of the Vaults: this is the chapel where St. Catherine donned her nun's habit of the Mantellate Order for the very first time, in 1363. Near the altar there is a fresco depicting St. Catherine by the 14th cent. artist, Andrea Vanni, a portrait which is considered to bear the greatest likeness to her. In the background, on the furthest wall, you will see The Coronation of St. Catherine, by Mattia Preti.

St. Dominic's Basilica
1: *A suggestive nocturnal view of the façade*
2: *Aerial view of the entire complex from the part of the apse. Below, Fonte Branda*
3: *The large nave*

The right wall: at the 1st altar: here there is a beautiful wooden Crucifix of the 14th century and a polychrome terracotta *Pietà*. At the 2nd altar, a beautiful *Madonna* by *Sano di Pietro* and the *Nativity of Mary* by *Alessandro Casolani*.

In the *Cappella di S. Caterina* (St. Catherine's Chapel), built in 1488, the embalmed head of St. Catherine is kept in a shrine.

There are also many frescos depicting scenes of her life.

Up high in the arch of the portal are *Saints Luke and Girolamo* by *Sodoma*, whilst below there is another fresco by *Francesco Vanni* that depicts the *Blessed Raimondo di Capua and Tommaso Nacci*. On the sides of the altar there is a magnificent fresco by *Sodoma* that portrays *The Fainting of the Saint* on the left and an *Ecstasy* on the right.

On the left wall there is another magnificent fresco by *Sodoma* that depicts the *Decapitation of Niccolò di Tuldo Comforted by the Saint*, whilst on the right wall there is an oil painting of *The Saint Liberating a Possessed* by *Francesco Vanni*.

The Vestry: near the door, *The Adoration of the Shepherds* by *Francesco di Giorgio Martini*; in the lunette, *La Pietà* by *Matteo di Giovanni*; on the Altar, *Our Lady of the Assumption* by *Sodoma*.

The Crypt: entrance is via a door at the end of the right wall.

The Crypt was built at the beginning of the 1300's, but was abandoned for centuries. In 1935, restoration works brought this beautiful Crypt to its original splendour.

The large room is divided into a nave and two aisles covered in Cross vaults that are supported by columns.

The large canvas by Sano di Pietro of the Crucifixion is situated on the Altar.

The right transept: at the 1st Chapel, *Madonna and Child between St. Paul and St. Catherine*, a beautiful monochrome fresco.

At the 2nd Chapel, the *Tombs of German Students* who frequented the University of Siena between 1500 and 1600. At the 3rd Chapel, the *Madonna between Saints Girolamo and John*, a beautiful triptych by *Matteo di Giovanni*.

On the Altare Maggiore, the masterpiece by *Benedetto da Maiano*, *Tabernacle with Angels Holding Candelabra*.

The left transept: at the 1st Chapel, *Madonna and Child* by *Sano di Pietro*. At the 2nd Chapel, *St. Barbara Seated on the Throne Amongst Angels and Saints*, by *Matteo di Giovanni*.

In the lunette, *The Epiphany* by the same artist. Opposite, *Madonna and Child and Saints*, and a *Pietà*, all works by *Benvenuto Giovanni*.

The left wall: at the 4th Altar, *Madonna and Child, St. John the Baptist and a Crusader*, a beautiful fresco by *Pietro Lorenzetti*. At the 3rd Altar, *St. Anthony Abbot Liberating a Possessed* by *Rutilio Manetti*.

In exiting the Church, to the right there is a magnificent 15th century Cloister with frescos by *Lippo Nanni* and *Andrea Vanni*.

St. Dominic's Basilica
St. Catherine's Chapel, with three magnificent frescos by Sodoma:
On the left wall: The Decapitation of Niccolò di Tuldo, comforted by the Saint.
Left of the Altar: The fainting of the Saint
Right of the Altar: Ecstasy of the Saint
The embalmed head of St. Catherine is kept over the Altar behind the grate.

On the following page
St. Catherine, by Andrea Vanni

2 - FONTE BRANDA

Fonte Branda lies at the end of Via S. Caterina beneath the Basilica of St. Dominic.

It was already in existence in the 11th cent. and was built of brick.

It has the appearance of a small fort with three merloned, Gothic arches and suspended arches.

The façade that we see today dates back to the last restoration undertaken in 1246 by Giovanni di Stefano not long after the Fonte was enlarged by Bellamino in 1198.

The Fonte Branda with the Apse of St. Dominic's Basilica above

3 - ST. CATHERINE'S HOUSE AND SANCTUARY

This is the house where St. Catherine lived. She was made a Saint by Pope Pious II and pronounced Patron Saint of Italy by Pope Pious XII in 1939.

Her fervent faith and the ensuing mysticism that surrounds her make her one of the most shining examples of Christianity. She convinced Pope Gregory IX, with her firmness of purpose, to bring back the Papal Seat from Avignon and restore it to Rome in 1377. Reading her epistles, one really gets the feel of the sheer power of her faith which enabled her to influence the authorities of her time to see her global view of the Church. The building that was turned into a sanctuary in 1464, features a beautiful Renaissance doorway made of stone surmounted by two elegant galleries decorated with Roman arches supported on slim stone columns. The room that was originally the dyeing-house for Father Jacopo was transformed into the Lower Oratory, the kitchen was turned into the Upper Oratory, the Saint's bedroom was called The Oratory of the Bedroom and the room that looked out onto the orchard was turned into the Oratory of the Crucifix.

St. Catherine's House and Sanctuary
1: The entrance to the house
2: The entrance to the sanctuary with the Portico dei Comuni
3: The Oratory of the Crucifix
On the following pages
4: The Oratory of the Bedroom
5: The Upper Oratory (ex kitchen)

Upon entering, we go directly up to the *Upper Oratory* with its beautiful coffered ceiling and golden roses, restored in 1594 by Riccio. There is also a beautiful 17th century meiotic floor. A beautiful canvas by Bernardino Fungai of the *Stigmata of St. Catherine* hangs over the Altar. On the walls there are 17 Renaissance stalls with 17 paintings that depict, beginning from the left:

1. *Jesus shows St. Catherine the Cross donated to a Poor Man*, of the *School of Sodoma*.

2. *St. Ambrogio Sansedoni*, by *Gaetano Marinelli* (1589).

3. *The Saint Comforting 2 Men to be Executed*, by *Lattanzio Bonastri* (1589).

4. *The Communion of the Saint*, by *Pomarancio*.

5. *The Liberation of a Possessed One*, by *Pietro Sorri*.

6. *The Blessed Giovanni Colombini*, by *Alessandro Casolani*.

7. *Jesus Exchanges his Heart with St. Catherine's*, by *Giovanni Vanni*.

8. *The Holy Spirit illuminates St. Catherine*, by *Rutilio Manetti*.

9. *The Canonisation of the Saint*, by *Francesco Vanni*.

10. *St. Catherine receives the Crown of Thorns*, by *Francesco Vanni*.

11. *St. Catherine has a Vision of Jesus on the Pillar*, by *Rutilio Manetti*.

12. *The Blessed Andrea Gallerani*, by *Francesco Vanni*.

13. *St. Catherine convinces the Romans to obey Pope Urban VI*, by *Alessandro Casolani*.

14. *Gregory IX leaves the Papal Seat of Avignon and returns to Rome*, by *Pomarancio*.

15. *The Nuptials of St. Catherine and Jesus*, by *Arcangelo Salimbeni*.

16. *St. Bernard*, by *Pietro Aldi*.

17. *The Saint donates her Tunic to a Poor Man*, of the *School of Sodoma*.

In passing through the gallery by *Baldassarre Peruzzi*, we arrive at the *Oratory of the Crucifix*, also known as the *Church of the Crucifix* as here there is the Cross where St. Catherine received her stigmata on the Altare Maggiore. It is an aisleless church in Baroque style with walls and ceilings frescoed by *Giuseppe Nasini*. On the left Altar there is the *Apotheosis of St. Catherine* by Rutilio Manetti. On the right Altar, *St. Catherine before Gregory IX* by Sebastiano Conca. In going back down to the ground floor, we enter the Oratory of the Bedroom with frescos on the walls that portray Stories of the Saint. Adjacent to the Oratory is the Saint's Cell where her personal objects are kept such as the stone that was her pillow. In going down further to the right, we arrive at St. Catherine's Church in Fontebranda, an aisleless church with cross vaulting. Inside, we can find: on the Altar, *St. Catherine*, and a 15th century wooden statue by Neroccio. The statue is surmounted by a fresco by Sodoma that depicts *5 Angels. St. Catherine receiving her Stigmata* is a beautiful painting by Girolamo del Pacchia. On the walls there are other frescos and canvasses that represent life scenes of the Saint.

4 - THE INTRONATI LIBRARY

The Library was built in 1759 upon request of the Academy of the Intronati founded in 1525 and is situated in Via della Sapienza.

The Library has a collection of over 300,000 books, incunabulum, manuscripts, codes, a 10th century Byzantine Evangelistary, a Roman Missal of 1456 and a 15th century Pontifical.

5 - THE CHURCH OF ST. PELLE-GRINO ALLA SAPIENZA

Also situated in Via della Sapienza, this beautiful Baroque style Church was built on an ancient Chapel of 1240 dedicated to St. Maria of Mercy and brought to its current aspect with restoration works in 1767. The interior has an aisleless vestibule and on the right wall there is a beautiful *ivory Tabernacle*.

6 - PIAZZA SALIMBENI

In continuing along Via della Sapienza we arrive at Piazza Salimbeni with its central monument dedicated to *Sallustio Bandini*. 3 important buildings surround the piazza: *Palazzo Spannocchi* to the right; *Palazzo Salimbeni* in the centre; *Palazzo Tantucci* to the left.

7 - PALAZZO SPANNOCCHI

Construction on the Palazzo designed by *Giuliano da Maiano* began in 1470 for *Ambrogio Spannocchi*, the treasurer of Pope Pious II. It is in Renaissance style with a smooth ashlar façade and rectangular windows on the ground floor, whilst the upper floors have mullioned windows with two lights surmounted by multigrade cornices.

There is a beautiful internal courtyard that was retouched by *Giuseppe Partini* during restoration works in 1880 and is ornate with galleries and capitals.

8 - PALAZZO SALIMBENI

This 14th century building is in Gothic style and was restored and extended by *Giuseppe Partini* in 1879. The stone façade is preceded by a short stairway that presents the ground floor with a beautiful Senese arch portal. On the 1st and 3rd floors there are mullioned windows with one light and Roman arches, whilst the 2nd floor has 6 large mullioned windows with three lights surmounted by Gothic arches that contain noble coats-of-arms. There is also a strong merlon over the cornices with hanging arches.

Today the Palazzo houses the Monte dei Paschi bank, founded in 1624 through the incorporation of Monte Pio bank

that was originally founded in 1472. The name derives from the fact that the Monte bank granted loans on the income guaranteed by the *pascoli marem-mani* (Maremma pastures), at the time known as *paschi*. Inside it is possible to visit the ancient storerooms of the Salimbeni Family.

9 - PALAZZO TANTUCCI

Also known as Palazzo della Dogana (Customs), construction of the building began in 1578. It is in Renaissance style and designed by *Riccio*.

Piazza Salimbeni
1: The monument dedicated to Sallustio Bandini
2: The Piazza

10 - THE CHURCH OF ST. DONATO

This church looks onto the square behind Palazzo Salimbeni. Originally built in 1119 as the Vallombrosion Abbey of St. Michael, in 1683 it passed to the Carmelite Order who carried out numerous restoration works.

The cotto and stone façade with a beautiful large rose and the lower part of the apse are all that remain of the original construction.

The interior is aisleless and houses works of art such as the 14th century frescos of the right wall and a *Tabernacle with Angels* by *Giuseppe Mazzuoli* on the Altare Maggiore. In the apse there is a fresco of St. *Michael* by *Luigi Ademollo*, whilst in the adjacent Oratory of Saints Chiodi we can admire a beautiful *Madonna* by *Andrea Vanni*.

11 - PORTA AND FONTE OVILE

Continuing along towards the walls of the city we arrive at Porta Ovile, the 14th century entrance. Outside the city walls, there is Fonte Ovile, built in 1262.

12 - FONTE NUOVA

We re-enter the city by taking Via dell'Ovile and arrive at *Fonte Nuova* of the 1300's, entirely in cotto with three large Gothic arches.

13 - THE ORATORY OF ST. MARIA DELLE NEVI

We can find this small building by going down Via Vallerozzi, on the corner of Via Montanini. It was built in 1471 in Renaissance style and designed by *Francesco di Giorgio Martini*. The façade is quite simple with a single portal and the Oratory has an aisleless interior. On the Altare Maggiore is the *Madonna della Neve*, the beautiful work by Matteo di Giovanni (1477) that gives the Oratory its name.

14 - ST. ANDREW'S CHURCH

Continuing along Via Montanini, we find this beautiful church to our right. Originally constructed in Romanesque style, it was completely transformed in the 18th century. The interior is aisleless with a single nave and there is a beautiful triptych on the Altare Maggiore by *Giovanni di Paolo* (1445) that depicts *The Coronation of the Virgin between Saints Peter and Andrew*.

15 - ST. BARTHOLOMEW'S CHURCH

Upon entering Via Camollia we find this 13th century church to our right. It has a simple interior with a single nave and no aisles, where there is the *Tomb of Pinturicchio*. The church also houses beautiful works such as a *Madonna* by *Sano di Pietro* and a *Madonna and Child* by *Vecchietta*.

16 - THE CHURCH OF FONTEGIUSTA

After having crossed the arch of the same name on the left hand side of Via Camollia, we find this Renaissance style church of the end of the 15th century.

It has a cotto façade with its portal contained in a marble cornice, the work of *Urbano da Cortona*. By the same artist are the high-relief works that represent the *Madonna amongst Angels*. The interior is of a square plan and divided into a nave and two aisles by 4 columns that support the decorated cross vaulting. On the entrance wall there is a beautiful stained glass window by *Guidoccio Cozzarelli* that depicts the *Madonna and Child between St. Catherine and St. Bernard*.

The Church of Fontegiusta
1: The Visitation, by Michelangelo Anselmi
2: Siena and the Plague, by Riccio
3: The central nave: in the lunette over the Altare Maggiore the Assumption, by Girolamo Benvenuto

17 - THE CHURCH OF ST. PETER ALLA MAGIONE

In continuing along towards Porta Camollia we find this church at the top of a long stairway. It was built in the 11th century by the Templar Order to be then passed onto the Order of Malta. The façade has a Gothic style portal and on the right there is a Renaissance style Chapel. The interior is aisleless with a trussed ceiling and it has a raised presbytery. On the walls there are monochrome frescos that date back to the 14th century depicting Biblical stories. In the Chapel there is a fresco of the Madonna and Child by Riccio.

18 - PORTA CAMOLLIA

This door to the city is made up of three arches in the long walls that surround the city. It was originally built in the 13th century to be restored in 1604 by Alessandro Casolani. The exterior of the central arch holds the incision of the Latin phrase Cor magis tibi Siena pendit, which means: More than its doors, Siena opens its heart. This phrase, now considered a welcome to visitors to the city, was written in honour of Ferdinand I dei Medici when Siena fell into the hands of the Medici Government.

19 - THE FORT OF ST. BARBARA

This powerful bastion, also known as Fortezza Medicea (Medici Fortress) was built in 1560 upon request by Cosimo I dei Medici who placed the project in the hands of Baldassarre Lanci. It is of a square plan with triangular spurs in the corners. In 1937 the terraces became areas of public gardens. In one of the 4 spurs there is the Enoteca Italica (Vintage Wine Stock) where it is possible to taste the superb local wines.

1: *The outer door of Camollia*
2: *The door of Camollia*
3: *The Fort of St. Barbara*

AROUND SIENA

Immediately outside the city walls we find ourselves emerged in the immense beauty of the Tuscan countryside with its endless chain of green and floral hills, vineyards and olive groves. Amongst all this splendour are the medieval Convents, Cloisters, Castles and Villas.

This mixture of nature and art is what makes the panorama unique.

We have pointed out the most important places and things, but recommend not overlooking the rest, as everything in this part of the world brings joy to both the eyes and the spirit.

THE BASILICA OF OSSERVANZA

This Basilica is situated approximately 2 km from the city when leaving from Porta Ovile. It was built upon the request of *St. Bernard* at the beginning of the 1400's near a hermitage where the Saint retreated to meditate. Towards the end of the century it was extended and re-touched apparently by *Francesco di Giorgio Martini*. After the Second World War, due to extensive bombing, it was restored to its original aspect. The façade is in cotto and preceded by an arcade.

The interior is aisleless with a single nave that divides into 8 Chapels. Some of the works of art in the Basilica are:

In the 2nd Chapel, *The Coronation of the Virgin*, in stupendous glazed terracotta by *Andrea della Robbia*.

In the 4th Chapel, the *Madonna between Saints Ambrogio and Girolamo*, by *Sassetta*. On the arch are some terracotta works by *Andrea della Robbia*.

On the right wall, *Saints John the Baptist, Francis, Peter and John Evangelist*, a magnificent polyptych by *Andrea di Bartolo*. *Our Lady of the Annunciation* and the *Archangel Gabriel* are other terracotta works by *Andrea della Robbia* on the triumphal arch. In the adjacent *Aurelio Castelli Museum* there is a beautiful loggia by Pandolfo, the reconstruction of St. Bernard's cell and other works.

THE CARTHUSIAN MONASTERY OF PONTIGNANO

Again from Porta Ovile, this Monastery is situated approximately 8 km from the city. Built in the 14th century, this Renaissance style Monastery is made up of a Church and 3 Cloisters. In the Church and in the 3rd Cloister we can find the remains of frescos by *Bernardino Poccetti* and *Francesco Vanni* that depict *Stories of Carthusian Monks*. The beautiful wooden choir stalls date back to the 1500's and are the work of *Domenico Atticciati*.

1: The Basilica dell'Osservanza
2: The Carthusian Monastery of Pontignano

THE CASTLE OF FOUR TOWERS

In exiting the city from Porta Pispni and taking the road of the Valle dell'Arbia we find this massive 14th century Castle. From the corners of the castle, the four towers that give the Castle its name stand out. It is of a square plan with a beautiful internal courtyard.

Near the Castle it is also possible to visit the *Church of St. Regina*, built in Romanesque style in the 12th century. Here we can admire the remains of 15th century frescos of the Senese School.

THE BELCARO CASTLE

We exit the city from Porta S. Marco and take the national highway that leads to Grosseto. In a deviation of this main road, on top of a hill we find this beautiful 12th century Castle surrounded by a lush green park. Some of the rooms of the Castle were transformed by the frescos of *Peruzzi* in the 16th century.

LECCETO

Not too far from the Belcaro Castle is the *Augustine Hermitage* of Lecceto that apparently dates back to the 4th century. The Hermitage was completely restructured to its present state in the 14th century. It is surrounded by a thick forest and has the appearance of a fortress made up of a Church and 2 Cloisters with frescoed porticoes.

ST. LEONARD ON THE LAKE

This is also an *Augustine Hermitage* only a few kilometres distance from the Hermitage at Lecceto. Its origins are of the 12th century in Romanesque-Gothic style.

The church is aisleless with a single nave and the apse houses a magnificent cycle of frescos by *Lippo Vanni* depicting *Stories of the New Testament* surrounded by musical Angels. The refectory has a beautiful fresco of the *Crucifixion* by *Giovanni di Paolo*.

PIEVE DI PONTE ALLO SPINO

In the same area it is possible to visit this beautiful Romanesque style church.

The façade is in stone and the interior has a nave and two aisles with ancient capitals on the pillars.

Outside there is the ex-Convent with the remains of the Cloister.

1: The Belcaro Castle
2: The Castle of the Four Towers
3: The Augustine Hermitage of Lecceto

CHIUSI

Mentioned also by Virgil in the Aeneid, Chiusi is a very ancient town, one of the most powerful of the 12 Etruscan territories ruled by a lucumon. It had the same destiny as all Etruscan towns, and in 296 BC it became part of the Roman Empire.

After being occupied by the Goths and the Longobards, it was first subdued by the town of Orvieto in the 12th Century, then it passed under the dominion of Siena.

The medieval centre is surrounded by ancient gates. In *Piazza del Duomo* - the Cathedral was built in the 5th Century and restored in the 12th Century - the mighty bell tower rises; it was a defence tower originally, and was transformed into a bell tower only in the 16th Century. In the environs of Chiusi, you can visit the splendid *Etruscan Tombs*, rich in frescos. Among them, are worth mentioning:

The Tomb of the Monkey
The Tomb of the Pilgrim
The Tomb of the Grand Duke
The Tomb of the Hill.

1: *The Bell Tower of the Cathedral*
2: *Church of S. Maria Novella*
3: *Frescos of the Etruscan Tomba del Colle*

CHIANCIANO TERME

Placed along the sides of the Chiana Valley, the pretty little town of Chianciano Terme is known most of all for its thermal baths, which are particularly suitable for curing liver illnesses. Chianciano Terme is made of an old part, probably of Etruscan origin, placed on a hill and still partly surrounded by ancient walls.

Here we find a nice Rocca (i.e. Fortress), the *Palazzo del Podestà* and the *Palazzo dell'Arcipretura* with the *Museo d'Arte Sacra (i.e. Museum of Sacred Art)*. The modern part, placed more towards the valley, is gathered around the four large thermal establishments and is full of gardens and alleys planted with trees.

1: A detail of the thermal baths
2: View of the ancient town
3: The city centre

MONTEPULCIANO

Even this town is clearly of Medieval origin. Among the main monuments in Montepulciano we see the 14th century *Palazzo Comunale (i.e. Town-Hall)* attributed to Michelozzo and the *Palazzo Neri Orselli* which contains the *Museo Civico (i.e. Municipal Museum)*. Even the 16th century Cathedral and the *Church of Sant'Agostino* by Michelozzo are beautiful.

1: Aerial view of the historic centre
2: The Church of San Biagio

PIENZA

The lovely little town of Pienza is placed on the top of a hill from which it dominates the Val d'Orcie and the Tresa stream. Its urban system, which is suitable for a much larger town, is due to the will of Pope Pius II Piccolomini who in 1462 changed its ancient name of *Corsignano* into the present name of Pienza.

On the central square rise the *Cathedral*, built towards the end of the 15th century on a project by Rossellino, the *Casa dei Canonici (i.e. House of the Canons)*, the seat of the *Museum of the Cathedral*, the *Bishop's Palace* and the *Town-Hall*.

1: The Town-Hall seen from the Cathedral
2: The Cathedral seen from the Town-Hall

1

2

SAN QUIRICO D' ORCIA

Even San Quirico d'Orcia is an ancient Medieval village which used to be the seat of an Imperial Vicariate. The 12th century *Parish of San Quirico in Osenna*, the *Praetorial Palace* and the *Orti Leonini* (a lovely park with beautiful gardens) are all worth visiting.

1: *The Leonini Gardens*
2: *The Collegiate Church*
3: *The Church of St. Quirico in Osenna*

BAGNO VIGNONI

This ancient village can be found only a few kilometres distance from S. Quirico d'Orcia.

Famous for its thermal springs, a Roman tombstone in the left wing of the thermal baths proves the ancient origins of the village.

These baths are situated in the centre of the town and even on the coldest of days, the water that comes from over 1000m deep gushes out at a temperature of 52 degrees, creating the vapours of a surreal countryside. St. Catherine frequented the thermal baths; a gallery facing the baths by *Lorenzo il Magnifico* is in fact dedicated to the Saint. The new baths lean against this gallery.

1: The steaming thermal baths; in the background, St. Catherine's gallery
2: Panorama

THE ABBEY OF MONTE OLIVETO MAGGIORE

We reach this splendid Abbey, approximately 9 km from Buonconvento, by taking the Cassia highway. The first part of the Abbey originates in 1313, when *Bernardo dei Tolomei* retreated here to lead a life of contemplation. The *Olivetan Congregation* founded by Tolomei followed the rules of the Benedictine Order and therefore, through time, the Abbey became a centre of art and culture.

Finished in cotto, the Abbey rises in the centre of a forest. Inside, we find the *Chiostro Grande* (large Cloister) built in the 15th century. This cloister is stupendous as the external walls of the arcade are frescoed with *Thirty-six Stories of St. Benedict* that make up the iconographic cycle dedicated to him. Nine of the stories were frescoed by *Luca Signorelli* between 1497 and 1499, whilst the others are by *Sodoma* between 1504 and 1508. There is only one other exception by *Riccio* in 1536. The church is also very beautiful with its magnificent carved and inlaid *wooden choir stalls* by the Olivetan *Fra' Giovanni da Verona*.

1: *A portico of the large Cloister with its cycle of frescos dedicated to St. Benedict*
2: *The large Cloister*
3: *Fresco by Luca Signorelli*
4: *Fresco by Sodoma*

1

2

3

4

133

MONTALCINO

This is a lovely town situated on a hill-top rich in olive-groves and vineyards from which the famous *Brunello di Montalcino* is obtained, that is regarded as one of the best wines in the world. Montalcino is overlooked by a mighty *Rocca* (stronghold), built by the Sieneses in 1361, dominating the valleys of the rivers Orcia, Ombrone and Asso. In the centre, the beautiful *Palazzo Comunale* is to be found; it dates back to 1285 and has a slender tower on its side. The centre also hosts the beautiful *Church of S. Agostino*, built in the Gothic style, and the adjoining *former Seminary*, where the *Musei Riuniti Civico e Comunale* (Town Museums) are to be found. A few km away, you can admire the *Abbey of S. Antimo*, built by the Benedictines in the Romanesque style in the 12th Century.

1: Montalcino: Town-Hall
2: The Romanesque Abbey of S. Antimo

THE ABBEY OF SAN GALGANO

The ruins of the lovely abbey of San Galgano built by the *Cistercian Monks* at the beginning of the 13th century are one of the rare examples of the Gothic-Cistercian style.

The Church, which is in the shape of a Latin Cross, is now completely uncovered and the interior is invaded by plants.

Of the annexed Monastery remain only some halls and monks' cells as well as the Choir.

1-2: Aerial views of the ruins of the Abbey

1

2

MONTERIGGIONI

The tiny Medieval village of Monteriggioni was built by the Senese at the beginning of the 13th century as a defence outpost against the attacks of the Florentines.

For this reason, in fact, it has the aspect of a fortress and it is completely surrounded by 14 towers and strong walls. Inside the walls rises a pretty *Parish* in Romanesque-Gothic style.

COLLE DI VAL D'ELSA

Situated on the ridge of a high hill, the town, famous for its production of handmade crystal, has developed on 3 decreasing urban levels: *Il Borgo, Il Castello, Il Piano*. The town saw a flourishing development during the Middle-Ages thanks to the nearby Via Francigena, and still retains its medieval mark. In 1592, it was raised to the rank of Bishop's See and City. Entering the mighty *Porta Nova* upstream and going along roads with Renaissance palaces on their sides, you reach *Palazzo Campana*, the entrance to the centre, called *Il Castello* (the castle), where you can breathe a medieval atmosphere thanks to the typical narrow streets - *Via delle Volte* in particular - with a variety of tower-shaped houses, palaces and churches from the 13th Century. Piazza del Duomo is surrounded by *Palazzo Pretorio, seat of the Archaeological Museum*, the *Cathedral* dating back to the 17th Century - where you can admire a Pulpit and a Baptismal Font by Giuliano da Maiano - and the *Palazzo Vescovile* (Bishop's Palace), seat of the *Sacred Art Museum*. Going downhill, you reach the *Baluardo*, panoramic site of Piano, overlooking the whole Elsa valley.

1: *Monteriggioni: aerial view*
2: *Piazza del Duomo: Palazzo Pretorio and the Cathedral*
3: *Palazzo Campana; on the left: Palazzo Comunale*

SAN GIMIGNANO

Placed on the top of a hill dominating the Elsa Valley, this lovely town of evident Medieval origin is renowned for its numerous *Towers* gathered in the historic centre and very close to one another. Today there are only 14 of the original 72 towers. Although San Giminiano is of Etruscan origin, it started to develop only around the 12th century when the famous *Via Franchigena* was built nearby.

The historic centre, still surrounded by strong walls, has its heart in a huge 13th century tank placed among the Medieval palaces and dominated by the *Torri Guelfe Gemelle (i.e. Twin Guelfi Towers)* and by the *Torre del Diavolo (i.e. Devil's Tower)* annexed to the *Palazzo Cortesi*.

Notice the lovely *Piazza Duomo (i.e. Cathedral Square)* on which rises the Romanesque *Collegiata* (or Cathedral) built in the 13th century on the ramains of the ancient *Parish of San Giminiano*.

The inside is divided into three aisles and it contains precious frescoes and works by the main local artists from that period.

The square is dominated by the *Torre Rognosa (i.e. Rognosa Tower)* domi-nating over the *Palazzo del Podestà*. Opposite this building rises the *Palazzo Pretorio (i.e. Praetorial Palace)* containing the *Museo Civico (i.e. Municipal Museum)* in which many precious 13th and 14th century works of local and Florentine artists are kept. Also see the imposing pentagonal *Rocca (i.e. Fortress)* built by the Florentines in the middle of the 14th century.

1: The Cathedral or Collegiate Church of Santa Maria Assunta
2: Aerial views

1

2

IL CHIANTI

This beautiful land with a rich historical background was also inhabited by the *Etruscans*, who called it *Clante*, from which the current name of the town is likely to have been derived.

This region is universally known for the homonymous wine, the *Chianti Classico*; it includes several whole towns:

Gaiole in Chianti, Radda in Chianti, Castellina in Chianti, Greve in Chianti.

On the other hand, the following towns are only partially included in the Chianti region:

S. Casciano Val di Pesa, Tavernelle Val di Pesa, Barberino Val d'Elsa, Poggibonsi, Castelnuovo Berardenga.

The whole region spans the provinces of Florence and Siena, between the basins of the rivers Arno and Ombrone; its boundaries are not well defined except to the east, where it is limited by the *Monti del Chanti*.

Although the *Regione Chantigiana* is not considered particularly important from an artistic point of view, it is worth visiting its villages, small towns, parish churches and castles set amidst marvellous natural landscapes.

1: Olive harvesting
2: Vintage
3: An old cellar for the "vinsanto"
   (sweet white raisin wine)

CASTELLO DI BROLIO

From its walls, you may enjoy a commanding view of the river Arbia valley. Its first settlement was built in the 9th Century. In the 11th Century it was acquired by the *Ricasolis Family*.

Thanks to its strategic position, it was alternatively occupied by the Florentines and the Sieneses, during the wars of the 12th Century.

In 1478 it was dismantled by the Aragoneses, but was reconquered and rebuilt by the Florentines few years later. Destroyed by a fire, it was rebuilt by the Ricasolis in 1860, with the same features that can be seen today.

The castle hosts the beautiful *Chapel of S. Jacopo*, dating back to 1348, and the *Cassero* (castle keep) with towers, communication trenches to go the rounds, and the *Sala da Pranzo* (Great Hall), adorned with Flemish hangings and an armour collection.

The magnificent *Cantine* (cellars) deserve to be mentioned; there you can taste and buy the vintage wines under the make of Brolio.

Going on to Gaiole in Chianti, you can admire the massive *Castle of Meleto*, built in the 12th Century but restored in the 18th Century, when all rooms were frescoed and a quaint little theatre was built.

GAIOLE IN CHIANTI

One of the 4 capitals of the Chianti region, Gaiole is situated on the road from Chianti to Valdarno Aretino. The Massellone stream runs through the town. The *Church of S. Sigismondo* has recently been built recalling the Gothic style.

In the immediate vicinity, it is worth visiting the *Castle* and the *Pieve di Spaltanna*, both from the 12th Century.

Going on to Radda, you can see *Villa Vistarenni*, a villa from the 17th Century rising from a high hill, where you may visit its peculiar cellars made out of rock.

If you continue your journey, you reach *Badia a Coltibuono*, with its imposing monastic complex which apparently dates back to the 8th Century, and which was definitely inhabited by the Vallombrosian Monks in the 12th Century. The *Church of the Abbey* in the Romanesque style is overlooked by the mighty embattled bell tower.

RADDA IN CHIANTI

The town is situated in the heart of the Chianti, on the top of a ridge 578m high, separating the valleys of the rivers Arbia and Pesa.

Its medieval centre is surrounded by ancient walls. *Palazzo Pretorio* from the 14th Century, today the Town-Hall, has a façade decorated with noble coats of arms and with 2 wide round-headed arcades. In front of this palace you can see the *Church of S. Nicolò*, preceded by a beautiful fountain and a staircase.

The church preserves has a wooden Crucifix preserved from the 15th Century. It is also worth visiting the *Parish Church*, built from stone and adorned with an embattled bell tower, and the *Franciscan Convent*.

1: Radda in Chianti, Church of S. Nicolò

EMERGENCY TELEPHONE NUMBERS

Emergency service	**113**
Carabinieri	**112**
Fire brigade	**115**
Road assistance (ACI)	**116**

USEFUL TELEPHONE NUMBERS (City of Siena)

State Railways	0577.280115
Medical Services	0577.299466
	0577.299111
Italian Automobile Ass.	800 869135
Town Hall	0577.292111
Police	0577.201111
Traffic Police	0577.757777
City Police	0577.292550
	0577.292558
First-aid Station	0577.280028
	0577.280110

TOURIST INFORMATION (SIENA)

TOURIST INFORMATION CENTRE APT
Piazza del Campo, 56 - ℭ 0577.280551
visiting hours:
 9/11-20/3: 8.30-13.00 15.00-19.00
Closed: saturday aft., sunday and Holidays
21/3-8/11: 8.30-19,30 **Closed:** sunday.

HOTEL BOOKING
SIENA HOTELS PROMOTION
Piazza S. Domenico - ℭ 0577.288084
visiting hours: winter 9-19 summer: 9-20
Closed: sunday.

PROMOTUR: Via Fontanella, 4
Parcheggio il campo - ℭ 0577.45900
visiting hours: 9.00 - 13.00 15.00 - 19.00
Closed: saturday afternoon and sunday.

HOTEL - (Siena)

ATHENA ★★★★
Via P. Mascagni, 55
ℭ 0577.286313
fax 0577.48153

CERTOSA DI MAGGIANO ★★★★
Via Certosa, 82
ℭ 0577.288180 - fax 0577.288189

EXECUTIVE ★★★★
Via N. Orlandi, 32
ℭ 0577.333173 - fax 0577.333178

JOLLY HOTEL EXCELSIOR ★★★★
P.zza La Lizza, 1
ℭ 0577.382111 - fax 0577.41272

PARK HOTEL ★★★★
Via Marciano, 18
ℭ 0577.44803 - fax 0577.49020

VILLA PATRIZIA ★★★★
Via Fiorentina, 58
ℭ 0577.50431 - fax 0577.50442

VILLA SCACCIAPENSIERI ★★★★
Via Scacciapensieri, 10
ℭ 0577.41441 - fax 0577.270854

ACADEMY ★★★
Via Lombardi
ℭ 0577.332440 - fax 0577.332409

AI TUFI ★★★
Via Massetana Romana, 68
ℭ 0577.283292 - fax 0577.284076

ANTICA TORRE ★★★
Via Fieravecchia, 7
ℭ 0577.222255 - fax 0577.222255

ARCOBALENO ★★★
Via Fiorentina, 32-40
ℭ 0577.271092 - fax 0577.271423

CASTAGNETO HOTEL ★★★
Strada Dei Cappuccini, 55
ℭ 0577.45103 - fax 0577.283266

CHIUSARELLI ★★★
V.le Curtatone, 15
ℭ 0577.280562 - fax 0577.271177

DUOMO ★★★
Via Stalloreggi, 38
ℭ 0577.289088 - fax 0577.43043

GARDEN ★★★
Via Custoza, 2
ℭ 0577.47056 - fax 0577.46050

ITALIA ★★★
V.le Cavour, 67
✆ 0577.41177 - fax 0577.44554

LA TOSCANA ★★★
Via C. Angiolieri, 12
✆ 0577.46097 - fax 0577.270634

MINERVA ★★★
Via Garibaldi, 72
✆ 0577.284474 - fax 0577.43343

MODERNO ★★★
Via B. Peruzzi, 19
✆ 0577.288453 - fax 0577.270596

PENSIONE PAL. RAVIZZA ★★★
Pian dei Mantellini, 34
✆ 0577.280462 - fax 0577.221597

PICCOLO HOTEL OLIVETA ★★★
Via E.S. Piccolomini, 35
✆ 0577.283930 - fax 0577.270009

SANTA CATERINA ★★★
Via E.S. Piccolomini, 7
✆ 0577.221105 - fax 0577.271087

VICO ALTO ★★★
Via delle Regioni, 26
✆ 0577.333555 - fax 0577.333511

VILLA LIBERTY ★★★
Via V. Veneto, 11
✆ 0577.44966 - fax 0577.44770

ALEX ★★
Via G. Gigli, 5 - ✆ 0577.282338

CANNON D'ORO ★★
Via Montanini, 28
✆ 0577.44321 - fax 0577.280868

CENTRALE ★★
Via Cecco Angiolieri, 26
✆ 0577.280379 - fax 0577.42152

IL GIARDINO ★★
Via B. Peruzzi, 33
✆ 0577.285290 - fax 0577.221197

LEA ★★
Viale XXIV Maggio, 10
✆ 0577.283207

PICCOLO HOTEL IL PALIO ★★
Piazza del Sale, 19
✆ 0577.281131 - fax 0577.281142

PICCOLO HOTEL ETRURIA ★★
Via delle Donzelle, 3
✆ 0577.288088 - fax 0577.288461

ALMA DOMUS ★
Via Camporegio, 37
✆ 0577.44177 - fax 0577.47601

BERNINI ★
Via della Sapienza, 15 - ✆ 0577.289047

LA PERLA ★
P.zza Indipendenza, 25 - ✆ 0577.47144

LOCANDA GARIBALDI ★
Via G. Duprè, 18 - ✆ 0577.284204

TRE DONZELLE ★
Via delle Donzelle, 5 - ✆ 0577.280358

TOURIST INFORMATION
(COLLE DI VAL D'ELSA)

LOCAL TOURIST BOARD
Via Campana, 43 - ✆ 0577.922791
visiting hours:
　　　1/4-31/10: 9.30-13.30　15.30-19
　　　1/11-31/3: 10-13　15,30-17,30
Closed: sunday and holidays

COMUNE: Via Campana, 18
✆ 0577.912111 - fax 0577.912270

PRO-LOCO: Via Oberdan, 42
✆ 0577.920389

HOTEL - (Colle di Val d'Elsa)

ARNOLFO ★★★
Via F. Campana, 8
✆ 0577.922020 - fax 0577.922324

LA VECCHIA CARTIERA ★★★
Via Oberdan, 5/7/9
✆ 0577.921107 - fax 0577.923688

VILLA BELVEDERE ★★★
Via Belvedere
✆ 0577.920966 - fax 0577.924128

IL NAZIONALE ★★★
Via Garibaldi, 20
✆ 0577.920039 - fax 0577.920168

TOURIST INFORMATION
(GAIOLE IN CHIANTI)

LOCAL TOURIST INFORMATION
Via Casablanca, 18 - ✆ 0577.749411
visiting hours: 1/4-31/10: 9-12.30　15.30-19.30

HOTEL - (Gaiole in Chianti)

CASTELLO DI SPALTENNA ★★★★
Loc. Spaltenna, 13
© 0577.749499 - fax 0577.749483

L'ULTIMO MULINO ★★★★
Loc. La Ripresa di Vistarenni
© 0577.738520 - fax 0577.738659

RESIDENCE SAN SANO ★★★
Strada Chiantigiana, 29
© 0577.746130 - fax 0577.746156

LA PINETA ★
Loc. Monteluco TV
© 0577.734051

TOURIST INFORMATION
(MONTALCINO)

LOCAL TOURIST BOARD
Costa del Municipio, 1 - © 0577.849331
visiting hours: 1/10-30/4: 10-13 15-17
            1/5-30/9: 10-13 14,30-18,30
Closed: monday if isn't a holiday

HOTEL - (Montalcino)

AL BRUNELLO ★★★
Loc. Bellaria - Traversa Osticcio
© 0577.849304 - fax 0577.849430

BELLARIA ★★★
Via Osticcio, 19
© 0577.848668

DEI CAPITANI ★★★
Via Lapini, 6
© 0577.847227 - fax 0577.847238

IL GIGLIO ★★★
Via Soccorso Saloni, 5
© 0577.848167

IL GIARDINO ★★
P.zza Cavour, 2
© 0577.848257

TOURIST INFORMATION
(MONTERIGGIONI)

PRO LOCO LOCAL
TOURIST BOARD
P.zza Roma, 21
© 0577.304810

COMUNE: Via Roma, 9 © 0577.373206

HOTEL - (Monteriggioni)

HOTEL MONTERIGGIONI ★★★★
Via 1° Maggio - Castello di Monteriggioni
© 0577.305009 - fax 0577.305011

ANNA ★★★
S.S. 222 - Loc. Fontebecci
© e fax 0577.51371

CASALTA ★★★★
Loc. Strove
© 0577.301002

SERAFINO ★★★
Via dell'Abbadia, 2 - Loc. Tognazza
© 0577.318242 - fax 0577.318388

TOURIST INFORMATION
(RADDA IN CHIANTI)

PRO LOCO
INFORMATION BOARD
Piazza Ferrucci, 1 - © 0577.738494
visiting hours:
        march-october: 10-13 15.30-19.30

HOTEL - (Radda in Chianti)

RELAIS FATTORIA VIGNALE ★★★★
Via Pianigiani, 8
© 0577.738300 - fax 0577.738592

VESCINE ★★★
Loc. Vescine
© 0577.741144 - fax 0577.740263

VILLA MIRANDA ★★
Loc. Villa Radda - S.S. 429
© 0577.738021 - fax 0577.738668

IL GIRARROSTO ★
Via Roma, 41
© 0577.7338010

TOURIST INFORMATION
(SAN GIMIGNANO)

PRO LOCO
INFORMATION BOARD
Piazza Duomo, 1 - © 0577.940008
visiting hours: 1/11-28/2: 9-13 14-18
            1/3-31/10: 9-13 15-19

Hotel Booking: Coop Hotels Promotion
Via S. Giovanni, 125 - ℂ 0577.940809
winter visiting hours: 10-12 15,30-18.30
Closed: sunday
summer visiting hours: 9.30-13 15-19.30
Sunday: 15-19,30

HOTEL - (San Gimignano)

LA COLLEGIATA ★★★★
Loc. Strada, 27
ℂ 0577.943201 - fax 0577.940566

RELAIS SANTA CHIARA ★★★★
Via Matteotti, 15 - Loc. S. Chiara
ℂ 0577.940701 - fax 0577.942096

VILLA SAN PAOLO ★★★★
Strada di Certaldo - Loc. Casini
ℂ 0577.955100 - fax 0577.955113

BEL SOGGIORNO ★★★
Via S. Giovanni, 91
ℂ 0577.940375 - fax 0577.940375

DA GRAZIANO ★★★
Via Matteotti, 39/A
ℂ 0577.940101 - fax 0577.940655

LA CAPPUCCINA ★★★
Via La Cappuccina, 46/A
ℂ 0577.940381 - fax 0577.942031

LA CISTERNA ★★★
P.zza della Cisterna, 24
ℂ 0577.940328 - fax 0577.942080

L'ANTICO POZZO ★★★
Via S. Matteo, 87
ℂ 0577.942014 - fax 0577.942117

LEON BIANCO ★★★
P.zza della Cisterna, 13
ℂ 0577.941294 - fax 0577.942123

LA RENAIE ★★★
Loc. Pancole, 10/B
ℂ 0577.955044 - fax 0577.955126

LE VOLPAIE ★★★
Via Nuova, 9 - Castelsangimignano
ℂ 0577.953140 - fax 0577.953142

PESCILLE ★★★
Loc. Pescille - ℂ e fax 0577.940186

SAN MICHELE ★★★
Loc. Strada, 14 - ℂ e fax 0577.940596

SOVESTRO ★★★
Loc. Sovestro, 63
ℂ 0577.943153 - fax 0577.943089

VILLA BELVEDERE ★★★
Via Dante Alighieri, 14
ℂ 0577.940539
fax 0577.940327

TOURIST INFORMATION (SAN QUIRICO D'ORCIA)

LOCAL TOURIST BOARD
Via Dante Alighieri, 33 - ℂ 0577.897211
open april-october   19/12-6/1
visiting hours: 10-13 15,30-19

COMUNE: Via Dante Alighieri,65
ℂ 0577.373247 - fax 0577.897591

TOURIST INFORMATION (PIENZA)

LOCAL TOURIST BOARD PIENZA
Corso Rossellino, 59
ℂ 0578.749071

TOURIST INFORMATION (CHIANCIANO TERME)

LOCAL TOURIST BOARD CHIANCIANO T.ERME
P.zza Italia, 67
ℂ 0578.63648

TOURIST INFORMATION (MONTEPULCIANO)

PRO LOCO LOCAL TOURIST BOARD
Via del Gracciano nel Corso, 59/A
ℂ 0578.757341

TOURIST INFORMATION (CHIUSI)

LOCAL TOURIST BOARD CHIUSI
P.zza XX Settembre
ℂ 0578.227667

CONTENTS

© Copyright 2006 by
Officina Grafica Bolognese srl
Via del Fonditore, 6/5 - 40138 Bologna - Italy
Tel. +39.051.53.22.03   Fax +39.051.53.21.88
E-mail: ogb@tuttopmi.it

Printed in the UE
by Officina Grafica Bolognese srl - Bologna - Italy

Photos by: L.Angeli, Archivio O.G.B., Foto Gielle